AF600701

Women's Activism and New Media in the Arab World

Women's Activism and New Media in the Arab World

Ahmed Al-Rawi

Cover painting by Alaa Al-Musalli

Published by State University of New York Press, Albany

© 2020 State University of New York

All rights reserved

Printed in the United States of America

No part of this book may be used or reproduced in any manner without written permission. No part of this book may be stored in a retrieval system or transmitted in any form or by any means including electronic, electrostatic, magnetic tape, mechanical, photocopying, recording, or otherwise without the prior permission in writing of the publisher.

For information, contact State University of New York Press, Albany, NY
www.sunypress.edu

Library of Congress Cataloging-in-Publication Data

Names: Al-Rawi, Ahmed K., author.
Title: Women's activism and new media in the Arab world / Ahmed Al-Rawi.
Description: Albany : State University of New York Press, 2020. | Includes bibliographical references and index.
Identifiers: LCCN 2019036158 | ISBN 9781438478654 (hardcover : alk. paper) | ISBN 9781438478678 (ebook)
Subjects: LCSH: Feminism—Arab countries. | Women—Arab countries—Political activity. | Mass media and women—Arab countries. | Social movements—Arab countries.
Classification: LCC HQ1784 .A6734 2020 | DDC 305.420917/4927—dc23
LC record available at https://lccn.loc.gov/2019036158

10 9 8 7 6 5 4 3 2 1

To my daughters, Wejd and Rend, with all my love.
You're my hope, life, and future!

Artist's Statement

Alaa Al-Musalli

Scheherazade: The Powerful Storyteller

Legend has it that a king named Shahryar, a heartless man overwhelmed with wrath and hatred of women, began to wed virgins every night then had them beheaded the next day. Hundreds of young women lost their lives until he wed his minister's daughter, Scheherazade, the well-read beauty who ended his deadly rampage. She captured Shahryar's mind through cleverly interwoven stories that she would start just before bedtime and stop halfway just before the crack of dawn, with the promise to finish the next day. Many stories of beasts and kings of bygone times lasted 1,001 nights, until Shahryar's mind and soul were completely taken by the powerful storyteller, whom he made his queen. This book cover is inspired by the Arabian Nights and is meant to show the patriarchal nature of most Middle Eastern societies, yet it also emphasizes women's empowerment, for despite all adversaries and violence, women can and will find their right places and achieve equality.

Contents

Illustrations

Figures

Tables

Preface

One of the main reasons I was encouraged to write this book was the gap in empirical research in this important field of study on women's activism in the Arab world. More research is needed, as rapid changes continue to occur and new issues to emerge. The book is divided into six chapters. Drawing from a variety of sources, the first chapter provides an introductory account on the social and cultural status of Arab women and the nature of the prevalent cultural values that exist in the Arab world. It also offers an understanding on the changing beliefs and values that the Arab world is witnessing, partly due to the emergence of new media technologies influencing the lives of people in different ways. I argue that technology is useful in creating change, yet women's agency remains paramount in achieving equality and social justice amidst the many social and political forces that resist such change. The first chapter concludes with a methodology section that explains the different approaches followed. In general, the book draws its materials from raw data collected from many social media outlets—among them Twitter, Facebook, and YouTube—and a variety of social science computational methods are applied to analyze the data. Later, proper contextualization and relevant theoretical frameworks are provided to assist in interpreting the data.

The second chapter deals with a number of leading female activists in the Arab world and how they strive to create sociopolitical change in such various aspects as sexual literacy, ethnic and racial equality, freedom, and human rights.

Each subsequent chapter deals with a particular form of women's activism—religious, political, social, or cultural—and how it is aided by new media technologies and manifested through popular online mobilization and awareness campaigns. Each chapter presents important case studies that are empirically investigated to illustrate the complexities and challenges of women's activism in the Arab world. I end the book with a short conclusion that sums up the main findings, predicts the future trajectories of women's activism and the role of new technologies in the region, references the limitations of the study, and recommends possible future research.

Acknowledgments

This book's genesis can be traced back to when I was teaching an undergraduate course entitled "Media and Cultural Context" (COMS367) from 2015 to 2018 in the Communication Studies Department of Concordia University in Montreal, Canada. The course included lectures on women's equality, social movements, and rights from around the world, and my classes consisted of hundreds of enthusiastic, passionate, and active students from diverse backgrounds. I believe writing this book would have been impossible without the rich discussions and debates I enjoyed in this course. I would like to thank all of my students for inspiring me.

I would also like to thank many people who have directly and indirectly encouraged me to pursue this research project, especially my wife, Alaa Al-Musalli, for her generosity and making everything magically possible, and my mother, Nawal Namuq, from whose life and struggles I learned many lessons that have helped me along the way. I also wish to thank my two daughters, Wejd and Rend, to whom I dedicate this book. I am eager to see in the future how my daughters, who have lived most of their lives outside the Arab world, relate to the many causes, issues, and concerns of women in the Arab world. I have personally witnessed the injustice, mistreatment, and harassment that women in the Arab world, and elsewhere, continuously experience, which has been another motivating factor for writing this book.

I would additionally like to thank the NGO leaders and managers, especially Dareen Hasan, Roula El Masri, and Thuraya Rufaat, who generously responded to my inquiries and answered my questions about their important feminist activities. Many colleagues, friends, and students have been supportive of this project in particular and/or my research and career in general, including the following from Concordia University: Yasmin Jiwani, Stephen Monteiro, Brian Gabrial, Elizabeth Miller, Brian Lewis, and Charles Acland. I also thank Maha Tazi, Taghrid Alhowish, and Aranzazu Gutierrez for the interesting discussions on feminism, women's issues, and social movements that I had with them. I thank Karim Karim (Carleton University), Oumar Kane (UQAM), Jeroen Jansz (Erasmus University), Jacob Groshek (Boston University), Amin Saikal (National University of Australia), Cecile Rousseau (McGill University), and Tareq Ismael (University of Calgary) for their general support through the years. Further, I wish to sincerely thank the staff at SUNY Press, particularly senior production editor Diane Ganeles and senior acquisitions editor Dr. Michael Rinella, who has shown continuous support from the beginning. Thank you, Michael, for the numerous positive responses to my endless inquiries and emails, and for your great patience and understanding. I also thank the copy editor of my manuscript, John Wentworth, for the thorough, detailed, and insightful feedback and revisions made.

Finally, I want to acknowledge that some of the content of Chapter 4 on women's movements and social media was previously published in a paper that appeared in *Information, Communication & Society* in 2014.

Chapter 1

Cultural Values, New Media Technologies, and Globalization

Each chapter in this book delves into a different aspect of contemporary social media, highlighting its affordances and the ways in which women from diverse backgrounds have managed to use these new technologies to empower themselves. As ample ethnographic literature is available on the cultural and social aspects of women living in the MENA region, this book focuses instead on mapping new media outlets and their roles in changing the lives of women. I argue here that new technologies are assisting in creating predominately positive change, though sometimes negative consequences appear as well. In this regard, I am not an advocate of "technological determinism" (TD), which refers to the way technology determines the development of cultural values, along with subsequent social or political structural changes, or even of "soft technological determinism" (Smith & Marx, 1994), which sees technology as having a more passive role. Generally speaking, the three prevailing positions on TD include "norm-based accounts," which explain TD as a "chiefly cultural phenomenon" independent of other social forces; "unintended consequences accounts," which regard TD as part of the "unexpected social outcomes of technological enterprise"; and the "logical sequence accounts," which view TD as part of "universal laws of nature" (Bimber, 1990, p. 333). Overall, I find debate over which account of TD is most influential to be irrelevant to my purposes, as I see technology as only a facilitator, where the real changemakers are women with agency and courage enough to create a better future for themselves. First, to provide proper context for the study at hand, it is important to present background information on the lives and challenges of women in the Middle East and North Africa (MENA) region.

Arab Women and Their Sociocultural Context

Gender inequality is regarded as a pressing issue worldwide, as global differences between males and females continue in terms of the human development index (HDI); the largest gaps are found in South Asia, where "the HDI value for women is 17.8 percent lower than the HDI value for men, followed by the Arab States with a 14.4 percent difference and Sub-Saharan Africa with 12.3 percent" (UNDP, 2016, p. 54). Gender inequality is regarded to be the "most severe" in Arab states. UNICEF cites numerous challenges faced by women in the MENA region, including in education, legal rights, equality in inheritance, and protection from child marriages. Many countries still lag behind norms that have become conventional in most areas; for example, Sudan has not ratified the Convention on the Elimination of All Forms of Discrimination against Women (CEDAW) (UNICEF, 2011). Further, the UN Women Report states that although women in the MENA region have property rights in marriage similar to those in developed countries, they do not enjoy the same inheritance rights as those that female spouses and daughters have in other countries. In fact, the inheritance rights of women in the MENA region are regarded as the worst in the world (UN Women, 2015, p. 31), as Islamic jurisdiction generally stipulates that a female gets half the amount of a male's inheritance (Ahmed, 1992; Engineer, 2008; Esposito & DeLong-Bas, 2001, p. 38). Judith Tucker asserts that the "privileged female access to property through the dower system was counterbalanced, however, by an inheritance law that discriminated against females" (2008, p. 138).

In addition, MENA countries have the largest gap in the world between males (75–76%) and females (20–22%) in relation to labor force participation. The world average for males' labor force participation is 77 to 81%, whereas for females it is 50 to 52% (UN Women, 2015, p. 76). Also, the World Economic Forum (WEF) frequently publishes its annual global gender gap report in which countries are ranked based on four indicators: economic participation and opportunity; educational attainment; health and survival; and political empowerment. According to WEF's 2016 report, all Arab countries lag behind the majority of other nations in the world. Qatar ranks first among Arab countries at 119 (of 144 globally), whereas Yemen, commonly regarded as the worst country in the world in terms of gender gap, ranks dead last (World Economic Forum, 2016). According to the 2015–2016 annual report of the UN Women agency, the average female adult literacy in the MENA region is 71.16%, with wide differences across Arab countries since female literacy rate is 44% in Morocco and 45% in Yemen but 82% in Libya and 89% in Jordan (UN Women, 2015–2016). The report pointed out how women's capabilities and rights are "economically, socially and politically disempowering" in the region with poverty influencing women's "education, health, economic access, participation and decision making, and human rights' enjoyment as a whole" (UN Women, 2013a, p. 13).

In addition, armed conflicts, sectarianism, civil wars, and the refugee problem in the Arab world drastically increases the suffering of people in general and in particular women (Al-Rawi, 2010), who sometimes have more responsibilities than males, especially when the latter are killed or detained (UNHCR, 2014). In fact, women are often employed as weapons of war just for being females (UN Women, 2013a, p. 13); for example, UNHCR states that the majority of Syrian women refugees feel insecure and isolated, while the situation of Syrian women under the Assad regime is considered by Amnesty International (2016) to be horrendous. Partly due to the civil conflict that erupted in Yemen in 2015, many Yemenis face serious humanitarian challenges; for example, there have been "an estimated 17 million people at 'emergency' or 'crisis' levels of food insecurity" since early 2017 (FAO, 2017). In Iraq, ISIS enslaved non-Muslim women and allowed them to be raped with impunity for rapists; revenge rapes were then orchestrated by Shiite militias against detained women believed to be affiliated with ISIS (Taub, 2018). In short, many women living in the Arab world face multifaceted difficulties in their lives, especially those from poor families or from war-ravaged countries such as Syria, Yemen, and Iraq.

On the other hand, for the situations of many women, slight improvement has been seen in the MENA region in recent years, as will be discussed in later chapters. For instance, in 2016 "Qatar, Algeria and the United Arab Emirates each . . . closed approximately 64% of their gender gap" (UNHCR, 2015, p. 20). Saudi Arabia has seen a 48% increase in the number of employed Saudi women since the year 2010, partly due "to petitions and legal reforms that enable women to work in formerly closed sectors, including law, to go outside unaccompanied by men, to exercise voting rights and to be elected at certain levels of government" (UNDP, 2016, p. 113). In the following section, a brief overview of the cultural stigma surrounding the female body is presented followed by the influence of globalization and the use of traditional and social media.

As stated above, the majority of Arab women face tremendous socioeconomic challenges in their lives since most, if not all, Arab societies are characterized by their gendered relations, spheres, and roles, which shape the way people live their entire lives (Sadiqi, 2006). Within such a context, the female body has a special status as it is connected to many cultural taboos, such as the epidemic issue of *'ayb* (shame), sexual freedom, and family honor, while the values of *hayaa* (shyness) and modesty are important norms highlighted in both offline and online practice (Stanger, Alnaghaimshi, & Pearson, 2017). In this regard, Moroccan author Layla Al-Sulaimani rightly argues that sexual literacy in the Arab world is nonexistent since it is regarded as a taboo associated with pornography. Al-Sulaimani believes that this kind of ignorance leads to sexual desperation that ultimately results in enhancing the rape culture and street harassment (HuffPost-Arabi, 2017c). Further, Egyptian scholar and activist Nawal Saadawi emphasizes how Arab patriarchy is represented in its obsession with women's virginity, resulting in some parts of the Arab world in a cultlike milieu (Ghanim, 2015) in which midwives are tasked with checking to confirm that a girl's hymen is "intact on her wedding night" (Cooke, 2015). (Note that this particular cultural practice has been documented in only a few Arab countries that do not include Lebanon, Iraq, Syria, and Jordan.)

In some Arab regions, the hymen is regarded as "the most cherished and most important part of a girl's body, and is much more valuable than one of her eyes, or an arm, or a lower limb" (Abu-Odeh, 2004, p. 155). According to Layla Al-Sulaimani (HuffPost-Arabi, 2017c), a woman is often labeled as a "slut" if she is not a virgin before marriage. In some countries, including Tunisia, social pressure on Arab women who dared to have premarital sexual relationships force some of them to pay about $400 (in US currency) to "restore" their hymens (Hassaini, 2017). Such practices indicate a social hypocrisy that exists in many Arab societies, where men are permitted to have sex before marriage, and to marry multiple wives (Al-Krenawi, 2013), while women must abstain from sex, suggesting that men are in full ownership and control of women's bodies.

In addition, many women in the Arab world have special status in society because they are expected to be protected and shielded from real and imagined dangers. The beginning of the 20th century witnessed many debates about the role of women in society in many parts of the Arab world, including Syria. In the early 1930s, some male leaders in Tripoli, Aleppo, and Latakia, for instance, wanted to ban women from attending movie theaters and entertainment events, as Hama's mufti had mentioned that cinema could corrupt women's virtues. This led to a partial leisure ban for women in 1939 (Thompson, 2001, pp. 205–207). In Saudi Arabia, cinemas have been until recently banned because they were regarded as unIslamic (House, 2012), while gender segregation inside cinemas continues to be enforced in many other Arab countries. The Egyptian cleric Yousif Al-Qaradawi, for example, "recommends that men and women should be separated when they attend cinemas" to "prevent Muslims from committing illicit activities in the darkened cinema halls" (Larsson, 2016, p. 95). Further, regular censorship of websites, including covering women's body parts in album photos (Lakritz, 2017) and banning sexually explicit (and sometimes implicit) materials in traditional media outlets, is widespread in most Arab countries (Sakr, 2010). Media productions perceived to "threaten the social fabric, traditions, and values" (Al-Samarai, 2016) are prohibited. For example, in 2011, the Kuwaiti TV series "High School Girls" was banned on all Emirati channels during the holy month of Ramadhan. Mohammed Hayef, a Muslim thinker, mentioned that the "series portrays Kuwaiti schools as dens of vice and corrupt manners, making the girls appear to be lewd and shameless" (Calderwood, 2011). TV drama, then, according to some, is expected not to depict social reality but instead to provide a false reflection of it.

Globalization and Women's Lives

The Arab world's increasing contact with the West through globalization, colonization, and the postcolonial period has enhanced women's freedom movements in the MENA region because these elements have assisted in establishing more contact with the outside world and created more awareness about women's rights. The spread of feminist ideas coincided with the writings of famous Muslim and Arab thinkers during the Nahda period (Awakening), such as Rifa'a Tahtawi (1801–1873),

Buturs Al-Bustani (1819–1883), Jamal Al-Din Al-Afghani (1838–1897), Muhammed Abduh (1849–1905), Qasim Amin (1863–1908), and many others, who called for giving women different levels of freedom so that Arab societies can progress (Haddad, 1984; Karmi, 2005; Zachs & Halevi, 2009). For example, the Iraqi poet Jamil Sidqi Al-Zahawi (1863–1936) wrote poems encouraging women to remove their veils, often citing gender equality in the West (Masliyah, 1996). In this regard, one of the pioneer Arab feminists is Zaynab Fawwaz Al-ʿAmili (1860–1914), a Lebanese female writer, who detailed the lives of 455 Arab women that created positive change in their cultures. Al-ʿAmili also found women to blame for their deteriorating conditions since they mostly saw "themselves and their lives from the perspectives and opinions of men . . . [and] that they came to recognize themselves only through them" (Traboulsi, 2003). Other prominent feminists include Huda Sha'rawi (1879–1947), who publicly unveiled, especially in her efforts in establishing the Egyptian Feminist Union in 1923 (Badran, 1988; Shaarawi, 1986). In the same year, the Women's Awakening Club, regarded as the first women's organization to be established in Iraq, was created "by a group of secular Muslim-educated middle- and upper-middle-class women, many of whom were married to political leaders and intellectuals" (Al-Ali, 2012a, p. 94). The Club was headed by Asma Al-Zahawi, Jamil Sidqi's sister. Several other Arab countries witnessed similar awakening movements, such as Morocco, whose feminist organizations emerged "as early as the 1940s during the French Protectorate" (Ben Moussa, 2011, p. 139). These feminist efforts in the MENA region coincided with the rise of women's press. Hind Nawfal, for instance, published *The Girl*, the first women's magazine in Alexandria (1892), followed by *The Beautiful Woman* in Lebanon in 1909, *The Bride* newspaper in Syria (1910), and *Layla* magazine in Iraq (1923) (Ibrahim, 1996, p. 11; Al-Rawi, 2010). The latter was published by Paulina Hasoon who with Maryam Narmah are regarded as the first Iraq female journalists, their careers beginning in the early 1920s (Al-Rawi, 2010, p. 77). In the following section, a discussion is provided on the role of globalization and local influences in women's lives in the MENA region.

Indeed, the increasing contact with the outside world paved the way for new types of freedom and change in the Arab world. In this regard, the term "globalization" has become an ambivalent concept due to its different and often opposing interpretations (Hesmondhalgh, 2013, p. 273; Siapera, 2012, p. 24). In this book, globalization refers to the compression of the world and its global interconnectedness (see Giddens, 1990; Robertson, 1992), which can be linked to the concept of cultural convergence and the increased sharing and exchanges of knowledge, information, and agreement on blending the West with the East. In the Arab world, globalization and cultural homogenization have some levels of impact on different facets of life, yet local elements, especially the influence of cultural values, remain powerful forces in any society. In other words, there is an ongoing process of cultural hybridization as cultures are regarded as hybrid forms of various elements (Canclini, 1995). Here, Arjun Appadurai uses the term "disjunctive globalization," which refers to the notion that there is no central cultural dominance for any country as there are multiple actors and forces, that are often local in scope, which shape globalization and its impact on specific countries (Appadurai, 1996, pp. 27–29). Also, Marwan Kraidy discusses the concept of hybridity in that all cultures borrow from each other, for various regional and global influences play roles in shaping cultures (2006). Kraidy's concept of hybridization can be linked to cultural diffusion (transmission) that occurs when a culture learns or adopts new ideas or practices from each other. For example, Femen, the global feminist movement, has become active in some Arab countries despite their general conservative nature. Some female Arab activist members of Femen protested the patriarchal nature of Arab societies by posing naked, such as the case of Amina Tyler from Tunisia and Aliaa Elmahdy from Egypt, who posted nude photos of themselves on social media to express their rejection of the misogynistic nature of their societies (Associated Press, 2013; Fahmy, 2011). The actions of these activists indicate that they want to reclaim their bodies by asserting their ownership, but they have created public anger, especially among conservative and religious circles. Kraidy defines Elmahdy's action as a "creative act of insurgency," with the female body becoming the site for activism and social change (2016).

Regarding the influence of globalization, Herbert Schiller (1975), Hamelink (1983), and Annabelle Sreberny-Mohammadi (1997) cite the concept of cultural imperialism to refer to the hegemonic Western cultural domination over peripheral countries by imposing cultural products, homogenizations, cultural synchronization, and the destruction of indigenous cultural values. In the context of this book, Arab women and their compelling issues and concerns are often linked to different aspects of globalization, for they are mostly viewed in the West "as a barometer for the success of Westernization, liberalization, and democratization" (Sjoberg & Whooley, 2015). The social media campaign "Muslim Women against Femen" is relevant here, as movement members equate Femen with Western hegemony and cultural imperialism in the sense that "foreign" social values are allegedly being imposed on Muslim societies without consulting them (see Chapter 3). A second example is related to a film produced by the *New York Times* in 2016 entitled "Ladies First," which deals with the social and political conditions of Saudi women by highlighting some of the challenges and injustices they face in their daily lives (El-Naggar & Bolt, 2016). The long video report highlights how the new mobile technologies assisted Saudi women running for political positions in the municipal elections to reach out to their constituents. About 980 women were able to run (out of 6,900 total candidates), though they were not allowed to use their photographs in their election campaigns or to talk directly to men (Stancati & Al Omran, 2015). The film was later accompanied by an online survey for Saudi women in both English and Arabic to get their feedback on various relevant issues (*New York Times*, 2016). As a reaction to this campaign, Saudis divided into two main camps. The first held antagonistic views, viewing the campaign as part of a hegemonic Western crusade linked to cultural imperialism. They also expressed clear anger and frustration against the film, considering it a distorted media production aiming at creating division in the Kingdom and tarnishing the country's image abroad. Some Saudi women tweeted comparisons in the treatments of women in America and Saudi Arabia, using the hashtag "crimes of America against women" (#جرايم_امريكا_ضد_المراه). In contrast, the second camp viewed the online survey favorably, especially those who supported the Twitter hashtag campaign launched by Saudi women on canceling the man's guardianship rule over women (سعوديات_نطالب_باسقاط_الولايه1) (Al-Turki, 2016). The hashtag, actively used by many Saudi female activists, including Manal Al-Sharif (see Chapter 4), is marked by specific numbers to document the number of days it started trending on Twitter.

In connection to the above argument on cultural imperialism, a number of Western liberal feminist organizations and groups have developed a sense of "rescue mission" to assist women in the MENA region, for there is an obvious "missionary zeal of proselytizing, converting, saving, and rescuing . . . [them] from their misogynistic Muslim captors" (Massad, 2015, p. 110). Most of the above efforts seem to be good intentioned, yet many feminist groups solely blame Islam to be behind the problems that women face while disregarding local cultural influences and the economic, historical, and political contexts. Marnia Lazreg, for instance, discusses the precarious position of Muslim women in the West:

> On the one hand, they have been represented as oppressed by their religion, typically understood as being fundamentally inimical to women's social progress. From this perspective, the veil has traditionally been discussed as the most tangible sign of women's "oppression." On the other hand, Muslim women have been described as the weakest link in Muslim societies, which should be targeted for political propaganda aimed at killing two birds with one stone: showing that Islam is a backward and misogynous religion, and underscoring the callousness or cruelty of the men who use Islam for political aims. (2009, p. 1)

Further, Afkhami and Friedl (1997) assert that there are various "local cultural traditions that historically cannot be justified with reference to Islam" (p. xiii) since each country in the MENA region should be examined separately because various aspects must be considered in assessing and understanding the different situations of women. As mentioned, Arab countries are not homogenous, despite sharing the same classical Arabic language, history, and some cultural values. Rather, numerous local and national factors shape and define individual Arab countries, such as each country's traditional views on marriage, women, sexuality, and homosexuality. Further, many cultural nuances must be closely examined when women's treatment is analyzed. For example, Hanna Papanek observes that women in Pakistan who wear purdah are not as seemingly persecuted or passive as many Westerners believe. "Despite its forbidding appearance, [the purdah] can be considered a liberating invention, since it provides a kind of portable seclusion which enables women to move out of segregated living spaces while still observing" their gendered rules (Papanek, 1971). Abu-Lughod agrees on the partial liberating function of the Purdah in Pakistan as well as the way the veil functions in other Muslim countries (2013). To give another example, the liberal Lebanese channel LBC aired a controversial interview in 2009 with a Saudi man called Mazin Abdul Jawad who mentioned how he used to successfully flirt with many Saudi women in Jeddah. He was later imprisoned for five years for publicly discussing his sexual adventures, while some of his friends received lashes for appearing with Abdul Jawad on TV (CNN Arabic, 2014a). Most importantly, Abdul Jawad highlighted in the televised interview how new mobile technologies like Bluetooth assisted him in flirting and establishing initial contact with women in public places like shopping malls. Incidentally, some women who wear the niqab (face veil) find it easier to establish romantic relationships because it is difficult to identify them publicly, for the niqab can be considered, in this specific context, an empowerment tool used by some women as part of their sexual liberation aided by new media technologies.

Old/New Media and Cultural Change

Though this book's focus is on new media, it is impossible to overlook or ignore the role of traditional or old media in creating cultural change, for many television and radio outlets have repeatedly challenged the status quo and traditional norms by presenting ideas that often discuss women's empowerment and equal rights. Indeed, they assist in changing people's social behaviors, norms, and interactions in the Middle East (Larsson, 2016, p. 111).

In this regard, Judith Butler (2004) refers to the concept of performativity, with a focus on repetition and familiarity, which shapes the foundations of gendered identity often replicated and highlighted in mass media. As Tuchman notes, there has been a systematic symbolic annihilation of women in Western media (1979), and Goffman has observed that women are mostly represented as sexual commodities in advertising through the ritualization of subordination (1976). Though there is a clear gap in literature on the representation of women in Arab media, the same kind of "symbolic annihilation" of women is widespread in mainstream Arab media, as the main focus is on their bodies (Al-Malki, Kaufer, Ishizaki, & Dreher, 2012; Obeidat, 2002). For example, the two liberal Lebanese channels, LBC and Future, which began broadcasting in the mid-1990s, "used women anchors in low-cut attire in a bid to woo Gulf audiences, who were unaccustomed to seeing women on their own television screens" (Sakr, 2007, p. 94). Numerous Arab female singers tried to use sex appeal to draw more listeners and viewers to their video clips, such as Rola's "I'm Rola" (2016) and Amar's "kiss my lips" (2017) (Abdulhakim, 2017). As part of the globalization influence, a number of global television channels have been launched in the Arab world, including SkyNews Arabia, BBC Arabic, and CNN Arabia, that can be regarded as a positive turning point in diversifying opinions, enhancing democracy, and encouraging freedom of expression, yet the values that some of these new channels spread do not appear to be focused on promoting gender equality. For example, MTV Arabia released several promos to advertise for the channel, and two of them are highly problematic because they clearly enhance the street harassment culture that prevails in many parts of the Arab world (e.g., see MTV Arabia 2008a, 2008b). Finally, there has also been an opposite trend that is concerned with assigning traditional media roles to women due to the influence of some powerful Islamic parties (Abu-Lughod, 1998, p. 244; Dönmez-Colin, 2004). These conservative voices are increasingly using media to spread their messages (Moghadam, 2003, p. 157) by insisting, for example, that women must wear the veil on TV, while many Arab magazine advertisements highlight gendered roles by featuring women wearing long robes (Al-Olayan & Karande, 2000).

Despite the problematic trends, many Arab female artists from Lebanon and elsewhere are, in fact, pushing cultural boundaries by disseminating unconventional ideas about sexual freedom, romance, and love in traditional media, such as the case of Haifa Wehbe and Nancy Ajram, who have become leading figures in the MENA region. Most of their music video clips and sponsored TV advertisements show seductive, partially naked, and sexually implicit scenes far different from traditional videos aired on mainstream Arab TV channels (Cestor, 2010, pp. 103–104; Abdel-Nabi, Agha, Choucair & Mikdashi, 2004). Indeed, these music videos, which often resemble Western productions, show the impact of globalization and the diffusion of ideas while also boosting the brand of the female artists and improving album sales.

Other media outlets played significant roles in spreading new social values and raising awareness about women's issues. For example, some news reports and concerns were voiced in the Arab world due to the potential impact of Arabic dubbed Turkish soap operas on young people, for these media productions have often been blamed, whether directly or not, for the increasing rate of divorce in Arab countries such as Egypt, Saudi Arabia, and Iraq (*Al Ahram*, 2016; *The Economist*, 2016; Hayatouki, 2012). Most of these TV series highlight the importance of love relationships and suggest higher romantic expectations that are different from customary notions of romance and marriage life in mainstream Arab cultures. Further, in December 2014, Sheikh Ahmed Al-Ghamdi, the former head of the Saudi Commission for the Promotion of Virtue and Prevention of Vice, brought his veiled wife for a televised interview on MBC to challenge the idea that Saudi women should publicly wear the niqab. Al-Ghamdi's decision was viewed as brave and controversial, and he subsequently received many threats sent to his mobile phone (Al-Awad, 2014; CNN Arabic, 2014b; MBC, 2014).[1]

As discussed above, the majority of Arab countries are patriarchal and conservative in nature, and women generally take marginal or secondary roles in society. This gap, in fact, can be observed in the online sphere as well.[2] There have been several attacks by religious clerics on traditional and social media platforms, especially in conservative countries like Saudi Arabia, and these types of criticism are meant to inhibit any changes that might occur in people's traditional social values due to globalization and the advent of new technologies (Alsharif, 2012). For example, the former grand mufti of Saudi Arabia, Abdul Aziz bin Abdullah bin Baz (1910–1999), issued a fatwa (religious decree) against the so-called different dangers of satellite dishes and new technologies because they air "various kinds of transgressions, immoralities, false beliefs, calling for polytheism and infidelity" such as showing "images of women, alcohol drinking scenes, moral corruption, and other types of evilness that exist abroad" (Imam Bin Baz, n.d.). A similar type of ideology is echoed by the current mufti of Saudi Arabia, Abdulaziz bin Abdullah Al Al-Sheikh, who stresses in another fatwa the dangers of using social media outlets and internet sites; he warns Muslims against accessing them due to the potential dangers that they contain in allegedly corrupting men and women's morals and spreading polytheism, apostasy, and moral degradation. For example, he points out that mobile devices can lead to "immoral crimes" because they can "facilitate meetings between girls and boys, exchange photos and phone numbers, and lead to illicit relationships" (Al Al-Sheikh, 2012). In other words, there is a clear mistrust among salafi (orthodox) and highly conservative Muslim circles in new media despite the fact that the same clerics often use these technologies to reach out to their publics. For example, Tara Fares, a young Iraqi female model, was assassinated on September 27, 2018, shortly after receiving death threats for Instagram posts and YouTube videos that were regarded as obscene in conservative circles (Hassoun, 2018). Though she never posted nude photos, Fares was regarded as someone who crossed the lines (BBC News, 2018b). I argue here that the killing of Fares is a form of terrorism because it creates an atmosphere of terror intended to warn other women to behave according to masculine conservative standards.

Within this difficult social context, globalization and new media technologies have assisted women in creating change in their lives by empowering them in a variety of ways. New technologies with their convergence and affordances have assisted in what is known as globalization from below, especially with the rise of transnational liberation movements (Brecher, Costello & Smith, 2000; Della Porta, 2006; Evans, 2012; Kahn & Kellner, 2004; McEvoy & McGregor, 2008). Many scholars have identified the way ICTs (information and communication technologies) have assisted in enhancing citizenship participation, political engagement, activism, and democracy (Deibert, 2000; Flew & Smith, 2014, p. 119; Postmes & Brunsting, 2002). Other technologies have assisted in enhancing activism, such as fax machines and photocopiers, believed to have helped strengthen the anti–Soviet Union movement (Brown & Duguid, 1996), while Usenet was used during the coup in Moscow in 1992, and SMS texting helped in overthrowing the political leadership in the Philippines (Rafael, 2003).

With the advent of social media, many scholars started referencing Habermas's notion of the public sphere more than before, as interactive social media sites tend to function as alternative media outlets for ordinary people (Al-Rawi, 2014). Manuel Castells calls this new collective and connective phenomenon the "global network society" that is "built around the media communication system and internet networks, particularly in the social spaces of the Web 2.0, as exemplified by YouTube, MySpace, Facebook, and the growing blogosphere" (Castells, 2008, p. 90). This global network society creates a participatory culture that offers new opportunities for online users to use horizontal modes of communication in which there is more peer-to-peer and equal flows of information including access, dissemination, and sharing (Castells, 2001). In this regard, ordinary users have more agency in this new networked society, for online messages can reach global audiences while their production is self-generated, self-directed, and self-selected in what is called mass self-communication (Castells, 2007).

In terms of the Arab world, the emergence of Arab Spring events has been increasingly mentioned as evidence of the impact of ICT on people's political activism, especially in connection to women's movements. It has been argued that social media outlets provided empowerment for women in different fields of their lives (Arab Social Media Report, 2011), especially with more than 125 million individuals using the internet (see Table 1.1) and more than 53 million actively using social networking technologies, as of 2013 (Dubai School of Government, 2013).[3] Through their participation in these popular protests, women have become involved in the fourth wave of feminism in the region (Almahasheer, 2018), developed with the assistance of technology (Zimmerman, 2017), for the "internet has created a 'call-out' culture, in which sexism or misogyny can be 'called out' and challenged" (Munro, 2013, p. 23). It is also claimed that a new image of Arab women has emerged in the West: "women who are courageous, independent, and technologically savvy" despite some of the leading figures being perceived as passive veiled women, such as Tawakol Karman (Eltantawy, 2013). For example, Esraa Abdel Fattah, nicknamed "the Facebook girl" and nominated for a Nobel Peace Prize, is another veiled Egyptian woman well known for her social media activism. She was responsible for co-establishing the April 6 Youth Movement that led to the mass protests that toppled Honsi Mubarak's rule (Greenslade, 2016). Also, the Arab Spring events showed how women from different secular and religious groups became united under mutual emancipatory objectives (Khamis, 2011) as their activities increasingly converged (Lewis, 2012) through a clear transnational feminist dimension achieved via the influence of globalization (Cooke, 2016). Further, the use of "modern information technology, particularly social media in the forms of Facebook, YouTube, Twitter, and smart phones" assisted Arab women in avoiding "stifling government controls" of mainstream media (Odine, 2013). In short, social media and new technologies allowed women to freely voice their concerns and to express their social aspirations and political goals during

Table 1.1. Internet & Facebook Usage in the Arab World*

Arab World Countries	Population 2017 (estimated)	Users, in December 31, 2000	Internet Usage March 31, 2017	Facebook June 30, 2016
Bahrain	1,418,895	40,000	1,278,752	800,000
Iraq	38,654,287	12,500	14,000,000	14,000,000
Jordan	7,876,703	127,300	5,700,000	4,800,000
Kuwait	4,099,932	150,000	3,202,110	2,300,000
Lebanon	6,039,277	300,000	4,577,007	3,100,000
Oman	4,741,305	90,000	3,310,260	1,500,000
Palestine	4,928,225	35,000	3,007,869	1,700,000
Qatar	2,338,085	30,000	2,200,000	2,200,000
Saudi Arabia	32,742,664	200,000	20,813,695	14,000,000
Syria	18,906,907	30,000	5,502,250	n/a
UAE	9,397,599	735,000	8,515,420	7,700,000
Yemen	28,119,546	15,000	6,773,228	1,800,000
Algeria	41,063,753	50,000	18,580,000	15,000,000
Comoros	825,920	1,500	60,000	60,000
Djiboutí	911,382	1,400	150,000	150,000
Egypt	95,215,102	450,000	34,800,000	32,000,000
Eritrea	5,481,906	5,000	71,000	63,000
Libya	6,408,742	10,000	2,800,000	2,800,000
Mauritania	4,266,448	5,000	714,132	370,000
Morocco	35,241,418	100,000	20,207,154	12,000,000
Somalia	11,391,962	200	660,000	660,000
Sudan	42,166,323	30,000	10,886,813	n/a
Tunisia	11,494,760	100,000	5,800,000	5,800,000
Total	**413,731,141**	**2,517,900**	**173,609,690**	**122,803,000**

*Data retrieved and compiled by the author from World Internet Stats (www.internetworldstats.com/stats1.htm) on June 18, 2017.

the Arab Spring event and afterward (Radsch & Khamis, 2013), and were especially useful in disseminating ideas (Rane & Salem, 2012) and reaching out to broader audiences (Gaby & Caren, 2012). Indeed, the degree of impact of the Arab Spring on women's lives varies depending on the unique local circumstances across Arab countries. For example, the general social issues that concern women in Oman, the UAE, and Qatar are far different in their intensity and urgency than those that concern women in Yemen, Iraq, and Syria. This is because the latter countries have witnessed civil wars and armed conflicts, which generally shape the social lives of women and their general concerns. The same argument applies to local and geographical differences. For example, Iraqi women who live in Kurdistan, which is relatively safer and more stable than the rest of the country, have different concerns from those of Sunni women living in internally displaced camps in Western Iraq, for whom the Arab Spring events had probably little or no impact.

Further, social media outlets such as #MuslimahPride, #FreeAmina, or women's communities on Facebook have provided women with opportunities to create their own online initiatives, such as mobilizing people for certain causes or social movements, that have proven to be extremely popular among users. At the same time, mobile apps such as "Know Your Rights," launched in July 2016 by Nasreen Alissa, a Saudi female lawyer, have served to empower women in the region. Using animated videos to discuss important and relevant issues such as "divorce, custody of children, inheritance and domestic violence," Alissa's app has been downloaded more than 50,000 times since its release (Alkhalisi, 2017). It is also important to note here that social media alone can never be solely responsible for the various anti-government protests that occurred in the Arab world, as mainstream media outlets, "domestic factors, and broader geopolitical contexts" remain very relevant and must be taken into account in understanding these protests (Rane & Salem, 2012).

Despite the numerous positive outcomes of new technologies, many challenges and negative impacts on users remain, especially for women living in the MENA region; these include harassment and threats online privacy (Dubai School of Government, 2014; Nihal, 2011). In an interview by the author with Dareen Hasan, the head of the feminist organization Nasawyia, Hasan elaborately discussed the online bullying against women that occurs frequently on social media; some of her views were shared by Thuraya Rufaat, the manager of Iraqi Women's Rights NGO (see Chapter 5 for more details). Hasan affirmed that there were fierce attacks against her public page and its pro-feminist messages and that "many posts were removed" by Facebook due to the number of users reporting them. Hasan revealed that she routinely receives insults, curses, and threats with sexually explicit photoshopped images, but stressed that these threats do not hinder her from pursuing her project. Most importantly, she has noticed a change in attitudes toward her women activism efforts, for obscene messages and threats have recently decreased, though some men continue to try to ridicule feminists' objectives and efforts in the MENA region.

Other types of negative outcomes include the increasing popularity of revenge porn against women and sometimes men. This is, indeed, not an exclusive Arab problem that is caused by the emergence of new technologies, for sextortion is well known to be widespread on social media outlets such as Facebook. However, the problem has been magnified in most of the Arab world due to its general conservative nature as "smartphones and social media are colliding head-on with traditional notions of honour and shame" (BBC News, 2016a). For example, the WhosHere app has been reportedly used by many men to sexually blackmail Saudi women after arranging private meetings with them in what is called "legitimate privacy" (الخلوة الشرعية) (Adan Al Ghad, 2015). Another controversial mobile app called Sarahah (frankness) that allows users to anonymously send messages to others has been increasingly used to "bully vulnerable people and spread hate." The app was developed by Saudi programmer Zain al-Abidin Tawfiq and became one of the top IPhone apps in the world in 2017 before being shut down (Griffin, 2017). In general, conservative voices who oppose women's freedom almost always equate moral degradation with intellectual liberation and gender equality (Al Haj, 2017), and new technologies are sometimes used to inhibit women's freedom, citing local cultural traditions "to deny women rights in the name of Islam" (Afkhami & Friedl, 1997, p. xiii). Finally, when using a Google autocomplete search in Arabic for "A woman should" (يجب على المرأة), we find that the majority of statements carry submissive connotations in relation to women. The autocomplete function provides an indication of the collective searches that people make on Google. The following are the main results: (1) A woman should obey her husband; (2) A woman should take permission from her husband in . . . . ; (3) A woman should obey her husband (different format); (4) A woman should wash; and (5) A woman should wash after sexual intercourse.

To conclude, globalization and the emergence of new media technologies have influenced many cultural values in the Arab world and provided new opportunities for women to become more empowered. Women have generally become more effective in expressing their views and better connecting with each other, yet social media have also inhibited some women, as many conservative circles use these new technologies to maintain power over women, often in the name of

Islam. Due to the influence of globalization and continuous international pressure, as well as internal calls for reform, some Arab governments have made improvements in women's lives, such as in the case of Tunisia, which recently allowed Muslim women to marry non-Muslim men and share equal inheritance rights (Cordall & Mahmood, 2017). This can be regarded as a good example for other Arab states to follow. The following section on the book's methodology concludes this chapter.

Note on Methodology

Several social science computational methods are used in this book, and this section attempts to briefly summarize them. In terms of data collection, a number of webometric tools have been employed in order to retrieve data from YouTube—Netvizz and Webometric Analyst 2.0 (Rieder, 2015; Thelwall, 2009); Facebook—NVivo's N-Capture and Netvizz; as well as Twitter—Crimson Hexagon and the Boston University Twitter Collection and Analysis Toolkit (BU-TCAT; Borra & Rieder, 2014; Groshek, 2014). In some cases, data collection has been done manually, such as in the case of some Instagram images. Metadata on social media use and number of followers is taken from SocialBakers and/or Crimson Hexagon, while the social networking analysis of Facebook pages was conducted using Gephi software.

Regarding data analysis, the textual examination of large data sets has mostly been conducted by using QDA Miner-WordStat computer software, which provides the means to find the most common frames, words, and phrases as well as offering visualization of the text corpus. The details of this software can be found in previous peer-reviewed studies that employed it (e.g., see Al-Rawi, 2014, 2015, 2016, 2017a, 2017b). Other approaches include using Microsoft Excel's filter and pivot table options to identify the most retweeted posts, most active users, and most likes and comments (e.g., see Al-Rawi & Fahmy, 2018). Selecting only the top posts is a well-established method in social media analysis because there is a lot of "noise," and researchers need to focus on what online audiences are primarily engaged with. Further, interviews with NGO officers and managers were conducted using WhatsApp messaging, email correspondence, and Facebook messages. All data analysis has been complemented through proper social, political, and cultural contextualization and theoretical discussion.

Chapter 2

Influential Female Activists and Sociopolitical Change

In this chapter we will look at how Arab women activists, opinion leaders, and thinkers use new technologies to create social awareness. I argue that social media has empowered these female activists and provided them with new venues to express their opinions, establish wider networks, and possibly influence cultural values. The focus will be on the social media outlets of four famous women, including Yemeni activist Tawakul Karman, who received a Nobel Peace Prize in 2011; Algerian novelist and thinker Ahlam Mosteghanemi, who created controversy over her feminist views; Nawal El Saadawi, a pioneer leader of feminism in the Arab world; and Nadia Murad, an Yazidi Iraqi girl who was enslaved and raped by ISIS and was awarded a Nobel Peace Prize in 2018.

Historically, many influential women in the Arab world in the 20th and 21st centuries created change and called for equality (Maktabi, 2011), as discussed in Chapter 1. Among these figures was Tuhfa Hable (d. 1995), who led one of the first street demonstrations in Ta'izz in the South West of Yemen against Imam Ahmad Bin Yahya in the 1940s to protest imposing taxes on people and prohibiting women from receiving their inheritance rights (Al Sharabi, 2014). In Morocco, Fatema Mernissi (1940–2015) was another prominent Arab and Islamic feminist and academic whose views have influenced many women of her generation, particularly her books *Beyond the Veil* (1975) and *The Veil and the Male Elite* (1987) (Devi, 2015). Mernissi stressed how a sexual division of labor was practiced in many Islamic countries, including males' control over females (Moghadam, 2003, p. 126). Other well-known figures from Morocco include novelist Leïla Slimani, who once described the laws in Morocco as "completely medieval, completely disconnected from reality . . . they ban sex outside marriage, homosexuality and adultery" (Agence France Press, 2016). Slimani strongly protested the mistreatment of two girls by their families and police after a leaked video showed them kissing each other. In Saudi Arabia, many prominent female figures have led movements against the former ban on women driving, as well as the male guardianship system (see Chapter 4), including Maryam al-Otaibi, who was once imprisoned for her activism (BBC, 2017). In Iraq, a number of women became socially prominent leaders, such as Josephine Hadad, the first Iraqi female pilot, in 1949 (Al Hurra, 2017), and Naziha Al-Dulaimi (1923–2007), female activist and member of the Iraqi Communist Party. In fact, Al-Dulaimi became the first Arab female Minister and made many important changes to the Iraqi Civil Code in 1959 to ensure more rights for women. Also, Sabiha Al Sheikh Daoud (1915–1975), the first female Arab lawyer and university graduate in Iraq, became one of the most important feminists in her time and in 1956 was the first Arab woman to become a judge. Her book *The First Steps into Women's Uprising in Iraq* (1958) emphasized how Iraqi women participated in the 1920 Revolution against the British occupation.[1] Daoud was involved in several associations and clubs that supported women's freedom and humanitarian work, including the Iraqi Red Crescent Society, Social Call Committee, and Women's Uprising Club, which held public debates on women's voting rights and freedom (Social Call Committee, 1951).[2]

Why focus on these particular four Middle Eastern women? Ascertaining the influence of some individuals on others is difficult, but the female figures included here have been chosen from a diverse group of people and from different disciplines and backgrounds, as they are regarded as influential on several fronts. In terms of the criteria followed, *Forbes* magazine, for example, publishes an annual list of the most influential women in the world, and usually two to four Arab women appear on that list; however, the criteria followed in selection are typically based on the individuals' financial influence or their positions in government, positions usually inherited through connections to the ruling families. Hence, Forbes lists have not been useful here. Another selection method is accomplished through observing the social media followers of women in the Arab world. By examining the top 10 social media female users in the MENA region in connection to the number of their followers, we find that the majority of these platforms are run by female artists, particularly singers, with only a few exceptions, mostly in Jordan and Syria.[3] Similar to a Forbes list, this method has not been completely useful, either. In the following section, a more-detailed discussion on the meaning of SNS (social networking sites) influentials or influencers is provided with a focus on offline influence and reputation.

SNS Influential

In general, "influentials" are regarded as "central both in the overall communication network and in the domain-specific communication exchange of protest messages: other users direct their messages to them in the hope that they will pass them on and help them reach a larger number of people" (González-Bailón, Borge-Holthoefer, & Moreno, 2013). Yet identifying influentials can be challenging not only in communication studies but also in marketing (Kempe, Kleinberg, & Tardos, 2003) and information diffusion (Gruhl, Guha, Liben-Nowell, & Tomkins, 2004). Defining "influentials" or "influencers" by assessing number of followers on Twitter and other social networking sites has been examined by several scholars (Huberman et al., 2009; González-Bailón et al., 2012; Kempe, Kleinberg, & Tardos, 2003; Kwak et al., 2010; Watts, 2002). Other scholars use three measures to identify influence: indegree, retweets, and mentions. Indegree is a reference to "the number of people who follow a user; retweets mean the number of times others 'forward' a user's tweet; and mentions mean the number of times others mention a user's name" (Cha, Haddadi, Benevenuto, & Gummadi, 2010). On the other hand, a few studies tend to measure factors such as TwitterRank, which takes into account "both the topical similarity between users and the [network] link structure into account" (Weng, Lim, Jiang, & He, 2010). Others believe that the dynamic processes occurring on a network must be explored by using social networking analysis, with a great emphasis on the role and positions of nodes and edges (Ghosh & Lerman, 2010), while some studies rely on betweenness, in-degree, eigenvector centrality, graphs, and visualization in describing the structural features of the social network and identifying the influentials (Borgatti, 2005; Freeman, 1978; Heer & Boyd, 2005; Hui, Crowcroft, & Yoneki, 2011; Mislove et al., 2010; Newman, 2005;

Tremayne, 2014). In this regard, Bakshy and colleagues (2011) state that influentials usually "exhibit some combination of desirable attributes—whether personal attributes like credibility, expertise, or enthusiasm, or network attributes such as connectivity or centrality—that allows them to influence a disproportionately large number of others, possibly indirectly via a cascade of influence" (p. 9). Finally, a few scholars caution that the influentials hypothesis might be somehow misleading since it "requires more careful specification and testing than it has received" (Cha, Haddadi, Benevenuto, & Gummadi, 2010; Watts & Dodds, 2007). To sum up, there is no universally agreed-upon method of identifying influentials, but in this chapter I have relied on offline and online fame.

In connection to the above discussion, Katz and Lazarsfeld's (1955) two-step flow theory of communication appears to be relevant here, as the focus is on influencers or opinion leaders. The theory deals with the way "ideas often flow from radio and print to opinion leaders and from these to the less active sections of the population" (Katz, 1957, p. 61). Katz and Lazarsfeld originally defined "opinion leaders" as "individuals who were likely to influence other persons in their immediate environment" (1955, p. 3), and this definition remains in use, more or less unchanged (Grewal, Mehta, & Kardes 2000, p. 236). In the age of social media, some studies indicate the theory remains valid in the sense that opinion leaders can generate interest and communication flow among ordinary people (Hilbert et al., 2017). For example, Choi (2015) relied on Katz and Lazarsfeld's theory to explain the influence of opinion leaders in South Korea who are more effective than online content creators. Also, Southgate, Westoby, and Page (2010) found that celebrity status or offline fame plays a crucial role in making content such as YouTube videos go viral. Several other studies confirmed that celebrities have a clear impact on making some online media content popular (Feroz Khan & Vong, 2014; Nahon & Hemsley, 2013, p. 78; Wua & Wang, 2011). Since most of the female activists or opinion leaders discussed here have previous offline and online influence and fame, it was easier for them to gather support for their social causes, as the role of "traditional grassroots activist" or "serial activist" involved in more than one movement cannot be ignored (Bastos & Mercea, 2016). In fact, this kind of influence corresponds with previous studies that found the need to have opinion leaders involved in a movement or cause to create some behavioral change (Valente & Pumpuang, 2007). For example, celebrities can be useful in creating awareness since "they are highly visible and already act as opinion leaders within society. Celebrities are also accustomed to being in the spotlight and thus do not have to be trained to speak in public or how to cope with added attention. Celebrities often enjoy taking on causes that are important to them to enhance their image and further solidify their celebrity status" (Valente & Pumpuang, 2007, p. 885). Among other advantages to having influentials in a movement is that they function as facilitators for the strong diffusion of messages through the broad connections of their networks.

Further, other studies on social movements and the role of influentials found a connection between information centralization and the tendency to have hierarchical structures in the network. In general, a "social movement can be characterized by the density and number of the connections that make it up. These can be strong or weak, and can vary in their centralization in several key individuals, groups, or organizations" (Johnston, 2014). It appears that centralization is one of the key points that shapes a social movement. For example, there is an indication that the opinion leaders in the May 15 (15M) social movement in Spain "emerge[d] spontaneously and minor actants devote[d] much energy to communicate with them (be it to have their ideas echoed, or to influence such leaders). This proclivity is coherent with economy of attention, i.e., the system tends to avoid the overabundance of opinions to prevent scarcity of attention. . . ." (Borge-Holthoefer et al., 2011, p. 8). To sum up, the female activists discussed in this chapter have clear offline fame and centralized control over their social media outlets that allow them to claim the messages they send and the causes they advocate.

Women Activists and Social Media Use

The four women discussed in this chapter are regarded as influential in their respective countries and MENA region (see Table 2.1 on page 24). Women activists have long been instrumental in several social movements that emerged in the Arab world, especially those who relied on the affordances of social media (Khamis & Mili, 2017). For example, Lina Ben Mhenni from Tunisia was the "only blogger to be reporting live newsfeeds from the Sidi Bouzeid Governorate" (Madani, 2012), whereas Asma Mahfouz from Egypt became both influential

Table 2.1. Social Networking Sites Cited in the Chapter

SNS	Likes/ followers/ views	Link
Mosteghanemi	11.7m	www.facebook.com/Ahlam.Mostghanemi
El Saadawi	159K	www.facebook.com/nawalalsaadawiofficial
El Saadawi	74K	www.youtube.com/channel/UCKQ0AYzr2F4nKYzdIj78xjQ/featured
El Saadawi	2K	www.instagram.com/nawalalsaadawiofficial
Nadia Murad	146K	www.facebook.com/NadiaMuradBasee
Nadia Murad	43K	twitter.com/NadiaMuradBasee
Karman	833K	twitter.com/TawakkolKarman
Karman	3.8m	www.facebook.com/Tawakkol.Abdulsalam.Karman

Data collected July 14, 2017.

and famous during the Arab Spring (Greenslade, 2016). Mahfouz was known for videotaping herself urging her countrymen "to go down to Tahrir Square on January 25" (Madani, 2012). Indeed, the activities of women activists became popular inside and outside the Arab world, and Sahar Khamis rightly asserts that the "prolific online and offline political activities of Arab women over the last several months have contributed a new chapter to the history of both Arab feminism and the region" (2011, p. 748). Social media outlets function as a virtual bridge that connects audiences with their favorite activists. In this chapter, then, we will explore the nature of some of these outlets since the four women discussed have a large number of followers.

To begin, Tawakul Karman (1979–), a Yemeni journalist and defender of human rights, in 2005 created the Women Journalists Without Chains NGO and organized several sit-ins and protests against the Yemeni authorities to defend freedom of the press in Yemen. Thus, Karman had moderate offline fame before the Arab Spring events. In late 2009, she was nominated by the US Embassy for the International Women of Courage Award for 2010. The US justification was as follows: "Tawakul's selection for the 2010 International Women of Courage Award would send a powerful message to the people and government of Yemen of U.S. support for the essential values of freedom of the press, protection of human rights and the promotion of women" (Wikileaks, 2009). Most importantly, Karman is the co-recipient of the Nobel Peace Prize in 2011 for her role in the Arab Spring in Yemen and the toppling of Ali Abdullah Saleh. She stood on a platform in Change Square and asked protesters to march toward the presidential palace (Solomon & Ghobari, 2011). As a result, Karman was dubbed the "Mother of the Revolution" and became the first Arab woman and the youngest person ever to be awarded the Peace Prize. She is also a politician and senior member of the Al-Islah (reformation) Party (Nobel Women's Initiative, 2011). Her role as a female activist in the Arab Spring has become a source of pride for her fellow women in the MENA region and beyond, as many revolutions have become associated with women's power, especially in Tunisia, Yemen, and Egypt (Al-Ali, 2012b; Khamis, 2011).

Tawakul Karman's Twitter and Facebook pages are both examined in this chapter. The decision to include her Twitter account was made to study the most replied-to tweets instead of the most retweeted posts because replies were far common than retweets. Since replying requires more time and effort than retweeting, it indicates active engagement on Karman's page. Based on the examination of 2,994 tweets that she sent, the results show that they received 72,167 retweets and 75,416 replies. The majority of her followers and those engaged on her page are male (79%), in comparison to 21% females, based on statistics retrieved from Crimson Hexagon. The findings show that the top 10 most replied-to tweets relate to politics, which indicate the kind of civic engagement Karman has, with a focus on two countries: Yemen and Egypt. In fact, half of the top posts deal with Egypt carrying a direct condemnation of the current president of Egypt Abdulfatah El-Sissi, who toppled the Muslim Brotherhoods' rule. Karman calls El-Sissi "the number one terrorist in the region," which shows her strong pro–Muslim Brotherhood stance. The same kind of politically biased stances in her posts applies to Karman's support for Qatar, which favors the Muslim Brotherhoods' regime. It seems that Karman's regional engagement in politics has also attracted the attention of different audiences; hence, her Twitter followers are mostly from Egypt, Saudi Arabia, and Turkey, which are predominantly Sunni. Her posts on Yemen reveal a clearly biased stance in rejecting the Shiite Houthi rebels, who are allegedly supported by Iran, in favor of the Saudi-backed Sunni rule in the country. As a matter of fact, Karman expresses a great deal of negative emotions and even trolls her opponents, somewhat of a surprise from someone who received a Peace Prize. This partly explains why her controversial tweets receive far more replies than retweets, as many responses contain insults and obscenities aimed at Karman.

As for Karman's Facebook posts, the top 10 most-liked posts are analyzed in this chapter. The results show that all the posts deal with Yemen, with references to regional powers Iran, Hezbollah, and Saudi Arabia. Other posts relate to self-promotion, especially regarding her meetings with and visits to various national and international officials. Again, Karman shows extreme bias in dealing with the Yemeni crisis. Instead of taking a more neutral stance, she publicly favors the Sunni rule of President Abdrabbuh Mansur Hadi, and condemns the Houthis, whom she regards as "terrorists" backed by Hassan Nasrallah, and Iran, whose alleged goal is destabilizing the region. Similar to her Twitter page, Karman's Facebook posts create a great deal of controversy and flaming because many users post insults and curses on her page. Incidentally, women and minority issues and equal rights issues are absent from Karman's top posts, as she is fully preoccupied with regional and internal politics due to her conservative and pro-Islamic views that are limited to supporting and defending Sunni Islam and the Muslim Brotherhood.

Second in our discussion, the famous Algerian writer Ahlam Mosteghanemi was born in Tunisia in 1953; her father was known as a nationalist who participated in the Sétif demonstration in May 1945. Mosteghanemi worked for the National Algerian radio in a program called "Whispers," which made her famous in her country. Afterward, she moved to France and married a Lebanese journalist. In France in 1985, she studied for a PhD at the Sorbonne; her thesis was titled "L'Algérie, femme et écriture" (Algeria, Woman, and Writing) (Biographical Encyclopedia of the Modern Middle East and North Africa, 2008). Mosteghanemi was regarded as the first female author in Algeria to publish in Arabic; her novels, including *The Memory of the Body* (1993) and *Bridges of Constantine* (1998), which received the Naguib Mahfouz prize in 1998, sold over a million copies (Ahlammosteghanemi.com, n.d.). A later novel, *Black Looks Good on You* (2012), became popular among feminists, with overtly discussed ideas on sexual freedom that inspired many women in the Arab world. Mosteghanemi was chosen as one of the most influential women in the Middle East by Forbes in 2006 and was appointed as Ambassador of Peace by UNESCO in 2016.

Mosteghanemi's Facebook page has over 11 million followers as of December 2016, and she uses it to address Arab women in general by providing them with advice on social issues such as marriage (Al-Arabiya, 2010).[4] On examining her Facebook posts, only one relates to women's causes. She had praise for former Algerian President Houari Boumediene (1932–1978), who was the first to post an Algerian woman as a minister and supported making military conscription obligatory for women in the army. Most of Mosteghanemi's Facebook posts are irrelevant to the scope of this study, as she is primarily concerned with Algerian nationalism, preserving Arabic language and culture, Islamic teachings, internally displaced people, and her personal life (she posts many images of herself). However, a form of activism does appear in her posts. In a message posted on December 10, 2016, she quotes from her book *The Memory of the Body*: "In the anniversary of the International Human Rights Day, human beings spend the first years of their lives learning how to speak, while they spend the rest of their lives with Arab regimes that teach them how to remain silent." This ironic post shows her obvious condemnation of the majority of political systems in the MENA region, which periodically resort to violence to silence dissent.

Similar postings are found on Mosteghanemi's Instagram page, where some of her political and social views are evident, with posts on the rights of Palestinians, poverty, and the condition of children in Arab states, particularly Syria. Mosteghanemi's regional interests in politics and culture have obviously expanded her network of followers, which could not occur if she limited her posts to one country, such as Algeria. Most of her Facebook followers are from Egypt, followed by Algeria and Syria. Again, very few posts are related to women's issues; one Instagram message cites a statement published in her novel *Black Suits You Well*: "Due to her utmost fear, she got liberated from fear. She decided to win the bet. She grew feathers where she expected to have two wings." This is part of Mosteghanemi's preoccupation with issues of love, passion, and romantic relationships, with a reference to women's liberation and freedom. To sum up, Mosteghanemi's social media posts contain few statements on women's rights, as she appears to be more interested in promoting other causes (as well as herself), but through her fictional writings she has become a symbol of women's liberation and freedom in the Arab world.

Third in our current discussion is female activist and Egyptian physician Nawal El Saadawi (1931–), whose views on female circumcision and sexuality became extremely influential in the Arab world, such as through her 1971 book *The Female is the Origin*. El Saadawi was herself subjected to female genital mutilation (FGM) when she was 6 years old, and later became an activist to make positive change in women's lives (Cooke, 2015). She is regarded as a pioneer in the modern feminist movement in the Arab world and in "radical feminism in Egypt" (Moghadam, 2003). Her translated books and ideas have had an impact on women's activism in other Muslim-majority countries as well, such as Indonesia (Nurmila, 2011). Trained as a physician, El Saadawi worked as a psychiatrist and university professor and wrote about 60 books, including novels and nonfictional accounts; one of her most important publications is *Women and Sex* (1972), which tackles societal taboos such as FGM and equality, which cost her her job as director general of public health for the Egyptian ministry of health (Khaleeli, 2010; Moghadam, 2003). She remains critical of Islam and other world religions, which she regards as oppressive patriarchal institutions designed to subjugate women. Her activism has resulted in censorship and death threats. Her name was included on a "death list" published in a Saudi newspaper, and "one evening, she even heard her name during the call to prayer: 'Nawal El Saadawi should be killed,' said the muezzin" (Cooke, 2015).

El Saadawi rejects women veiling, which she regards as a form of oppression, but she also stands against nakedness in the Western world, considering it another form of anti-female aggression; she states: "women are sex objects in the free market. I am against makeup. Plastic surgery is a postmodern veil" (Rubin, 2011). In the 1990s, she established the Egyptian Chapter of the Global Solidarity for Secular Society as well as the Arab Women's Solidarity Association, which included hundreds of women members but ultimately was banned by Hosni Mubarak's wife (Khaleeli, 2010; Rubin, 2011). El Saadawi is regarded as "the first woman in Egyptian history to be threatened with a forced divorce for expressing her views," particularly concerning her criticism of Islamic practices such as pilgrimage, which she considers to be a pagan tradition (Lloyd-Davies, 2001). She believes that men "cannot stand an experienced and intelligent woman . . . the experience and intelligence are a menace to [the] patriarchal class structure, and in turn, a menace to the false position in which man is placed, the position of king or demi-God in his relations with women" (as cited in Cheref, 2010, p. 73; Saadawi, 1982, p. 77). For El Saadawi, feminism is about "social justice, political justice, sexual justice" (Khaleeli, 2010). Despite some success in achieving positive change, including the criminalization of FGM in Egypt, she believes that oppressive practices such as FGM remain prevalent: "You can't change such a deep-rooted habit by passing a law. You need education. The law was passed to satisfy the west. They wanted to cover that disgrace, not to eradicate the practice itself. You have to change the minds of the mothers and fathers and even of the girls themselves, who have been brainwashed to accept it" (Cooke, 2015). During the Arab Spring events, El Saadawi was among the first to go onto Cairo streets to protest Mubarak's regime, telling an account of her experience at that time: "The young men hugged and kissed me . . . They tell me, 'You were our inspiration to do this revolution.' Even young men in the Muslim Brothers said, 'Thank you for your books—we respect you' " (Rubin, 2011).

Regarding El Saadawi's social media activism, she runs four main platforms, including a YouTube channel and Google+ and Instagram accounts wherein images related to the promotion of her activities, talks, and interviews as well as excerpts from her books are posted in both English and Arabic to increase her audience outreach. As for her Facebook page, her followers are mostly from Egypt, Tunisia, and Morocco, respectively, indicating her regional popularity. All of El Saadawi's social media posts are related to empowering women, challenging patriarchal authorities, and criticizing the overwhelming role of religion in women's lives. Her most-liked Facebook post, which is also the 10th most-commented-on post, contains the following statement in Arabic: "What protected me is my work. What made me strong is my work, my production, and my mind. It has nothing to do with the husband [figure] because he does not protect as he is ready to desert me for a [sexual] impulse." This is an indirect reference to El Saadawi's third husband, whom she stayed with for 43 years but later divorced after accusing him of infidelity. El Saadawi here is generalizing by saying that men in general are driven by sexual desires more than faith and loyalty. Other popular posts are relatively long excerpts from her novels and books, though short statements are also available. For example, her sixth most-liked post states:

> My brother, who was older than me, tried to slap me, so I raised my hand higher than his own and slapped him, instead.
>
> When my husband wanted to erase my existence, I erased his existence from my life.
>
> When my second husband cried: "Choose either your husband or your writings," I responded, "My writings," so we divorced.
>
> When the dismayed Minister of Health stated: "Obey orders or get fired." I replied "[I choose] fired!"

This post is an example of El Saadawi's typical line of thought: defying patriarchal authority and men's power because she regards life as a continuous struggle to achieve justice and equality. In her frequent attacks against religion, she is critical of highly devout women. For instance, her ninth most-liked post states: "The [female belly] dancer views herself as a sexual object, and she exhibits herself to be traded with. The Niqabi woman also views herself as a sexual object, but she does not want to exhibit herself, so she hides herself from others. A real woman does not view herself as a sexual object because she regards herself as a normal human being. She neither exhibits herself nor hides from others because she acts like a human." Interestingly, El Saadawi connects with her audience not only through social media, but also consults them on several issues, especially those related to popular protests, and she sometimes creates online polls to gauge her followers' opinions on matters such as their preferred topic to be discussed during upcoming public gatherings. In brief, El-Saadawi has been an influential female figure for many decades, her impact reaching several regions in the Islamic world. She actively uses social media to expand her activism and audience outreach.

Our fourth and final female activist examined in the chapter is Nadia Murad Basee Taha (1993–), a young Iraqi human rights defender from the Yazidi religious community. Murad was born in the small village of Kocho in Sinjar, northern Iraq. While she was still in secondary school, ISIS (Islamic State of Iraq and Syria) managed to advance to Mosul and take over her village in early August 2014. The terrorist group killed men and elderly women, while girls were enslaved; 18 members of Murad's family were either killed or went missing. She was taken by ISIS as a captive and was imprisoned, tortured, and used as a sex slave (Withnall, 2016). After managing to escape from her captors with the help of an Iraqi family, she established Nadia Initiative (www.nadia-murad.com) with the assistance of international organizations and foreign governments, as well as Yazda, a nonprofit NGO that helps Yazidi survivors of genocide (Alter, 2015). She addressed the UN Security Council and was legally assisted by human rights lawyer Amal Clooney (Buffon & Allison, 2016), who is of Lebanese-British origins. Murad was included in the 30 under 30 Immigrants category of *Forbes* magazine and was a Nobel Peace Prize Nominee in 2016 and a Goodwill Ambassador for the United Nations for the Dignity of Survivors of Human Trafficking (Moradi & Anderson, 2016). She was also chosen by *Time* magazine in 2016 as one of the top 100 most influential people in the world. Her activism is intersectional because it is not solely about women but also connects to ethnicity and religion. In 2018, she shared the Nobel Peace Prize with Denis Mukwege for their efforts in combating sexual violence during times of war (Smith-Spark, 2018). Murad became the first Iraqi to receive a Nobel Peace Prize.

Murad's efforts to raise awareness to the plight of Yazidi women and her community appear to be heavily reliant on social media. She is also obviously trying to connect the Yazidi community living in diaspora with others living in Iraq and elsewhere through the use of social media. Her Facebook followers are mostly from Iraq, followed by Germany and Egypt, indicating the international and regional scope of her influence. Her top 10 most-liked posts contain primarily images of her meetings with foreign officials, including former Vice President Joe Biden, former Secretary General Ban Ki-Moon, German Chancellor Angela Merkel, and Canadian Prime Minister Justin Trudeau. Her third most-liked post, also her third most commented on, is her announcement that the Global Justice Center in New York and the International Criminal Court received Yazda's official request to regard the murder of thousands of Yazidis by ISIS as genocide. The request was later approved, making Murad's mission more successful. Her other achievements include printing her name on Barcelona Football Club shirts in coordination with UNICEF, which is her eighth most-liked post and fourth most commented on. Murad writes: "My goal is to make football as a platform for supporting victims of human trafficking and minorities under endanger [*sic*]." She uses multiple social media outlets integrated together to maximize her audience outreach and impact and to send messages with intersectional issues. For example, she often uses hashtags in different languages—Arabic, Kurdish, English—while images posted on Facebook also appear on her Twitter account.

In relation to Twitter use, Murad mostly tweets in English, and the main recurrent themes are fighting ISIS, protecting the rights of Yazidis, and promoting her human rights activities. For example, Murad's third most-retweeted post mentions the following in Arabic: "Every hero who fights Daesh in Mosul is my brother and I regard him as someone sacrificing his life for my sake and honor. I was a slave in Mosul and today out [Iraqi] troops are liberating this land from those monsters who have no honor." As can be clearly seen, Murad's activism is focused on assisting her community members and preventing another genocide from happening, with a special focus on the plight of girls enslaved and raped by ISIS. Indeed, she has achieved significant progress, as she has managed to popularize her cause and inform different levels of the international community about the humanitarian crisis that occurs in Iraq and Syria. Social media outlets have helped her a great deal in connecting with sympathetic audiences to gain official and public support, and the killing of Yazidis in Iraq was finally recognized as genocide by the United Nations.

To conclude, the four female activists discussed in this chapter have been influential in their regions and countries and have established wide offline fame, as millions of people follow them on social media. As stated earlier, influentials are central to the information diffusion required to raise awareness about pressing women's issues. It can be quite difficult for most individuals to mobilize an online public, as they lack the offline fame possessed by the four women examined in this chapter. These four women are opinion leaders aided by new media technologies with a goal of creating positive change in women's lives (Katz, 1957). Interestingly, Karman and Mosteghanemi both worked or started their careers as journalists, after which they either changed their jobs or continued their original profession. Indeed, all of the women covered here are regarded as activists, cultural intermediaries, and powerful social forces due to their intellectual influence, broad networks, and strong outreach. Yet they are all limited, sometimes even biased, in their writings, which partly explains why some of them, particularly Karman, are trolled and flamed by certain audiences. Despite being females, the issues of women's rights and equality are not always highlighted in the social media posts of Karman and Mosteghanemi; instead, regional events and sometimes internal politics are far more prominent. El Saadawi is an exception in this regard due to her lifelong activism in women's issues, whereas Murad's focus is more on protecting her own community members, especially young girls, from genocide and rape promoted by radical Islamic ideologies such as ISIS. Drawing social media audiences has also become a source of pride and social esteem, as Mosteghanemi, in particular, frequently boasts about the increasing number of followers that she has gained. What appears certain is that new media technologies further empowered these female influentials because they can instantaneously connect with their audiences and freely advocate for causes and concerns in a way that was never possible before the emergence of social media.

Chapter 3

Religious Activism and Online Communities

In this chapter we explore how new media has provided a venue for religious expression and empowerment. I argue that online women's groups are an extension of offline religious practices, and Islamic feminism is not homogenous, as there is a clear spectrum along which different online communities exist based on the kind of adhered religious beliefs. More importantly, these communities practice a form of religious activism in pursuit of promoting particular religious values. As discussed in Chapter 1, veiling has been viewed by many Western critics and scholars as oppressive, yet veiling can be liberating for some Muslim women as a way of asserting their religious identity, devotion, or faith or expressing their modesty. In contrast, some Muslim women who decline wearing the veil argue that they are asserting their gender identity by refusing to blindly follow some religious edicts, while at the same expressing their affiliation with and connection to Islam. As long as these parties are not forced to veil or unveil, they can both assert their freedom, choice, and affiliation to Islam in different manners, and can both regard their actions as form of resistance and/or activism. This is a form of activism because each party resists what they perceive to be oppressive forces that try to alter their beliefs or change their behaviors. In general, the veil remains a largely politicized issue much discussed among Western politicians in connection to Muslim immigrants' integration into Western societies, and often referenced as a form of Muslim women's bondage and link to a regressive medieval ideology, indirectly suggesting the superiority of Western societies and the cultural clash with foreigners.

In this regard, Islamic feminism has been discussed for decades, and is typically defined as a "feminist discourse and practice articulated within an Islamic paradigm" (Badran, 2013, p. 242). Since this term is relative, it is generally defined in terms of the way Islam empowers women to become better human beings provided they identify with it and/or observe "some" of its teachings. As Azza Karam argues (1998), three types of feminism—secular, Muslim, and Islamist—compete amongst each other in contemporary Egypt. However, this triangulation appears to be too broad, as further levels of religious practice align along a wider spectrum; Islamic feminism is not homogenous, with diverse and sometimes opposing ways of manifesting it, especially on social media. In other words, for each type of feminism highlighted by Karam, one can find a spectrum of varying online communities that can be further categorized based on the level of their religious beliefs. In this context, El-Nawawy and Khamis believe that the "existence of different feminisms in the Muslim world is in itself another manifestation of the various views, practices, and applications of the notion of 'pluralism' within multiple Islamic public spheres today" (2009, p. 107).

To illustrate this discussion visually, an image from the Facebook page "My Hijab is My Salvation" shows different ways Muslim women cover themselves, and each type carries with it a certain mindset (see Figure 3.1). This is related to the fact that Islam itself is never homogenous, as there are different doctrines as well as "observant and non-observant-conservative, fundamentalist, reformist, secular, mainstream, . . . [and] religious extremist" (Esposito & Mogahed, 2007, p. 3). All of these women and feminists' groups, especially the Islamic and secular ones, "have discussed, debated, and exchanged ideas" long before the advent of social media, accomplished primarily "through the media, especially in the lively and prodigious women's press" (Moghadam, 2003, p. 219).

On one side of this spectrum, we find a strict version of Islamist feminists, such as Niqabi salafist women, who constitute a minority in all Muslim countries and view wearing the niqab as a duty toward Allah, for the niqab is perceived as a tool empowering one in becoming closer to God (see the online group "Niqabi yes, Complicated no"). For such women, Islamic feminism is not about achieving gender equality, especially since they largely believe that a woman is regarded as "*awra*" (shame) that must be well covered and concealed from others. Instead, Islamic feminism is more about strictly observing religious duties as well

Figure 3.1. Image from Facebook page "My Hijab Is My Salvation." The image contains two verses from the Quran with a question "Where is it going?" The first verse in the top is about a statement to human beings about the need to be protected from the Devil for his attempts to seduce people to leave Heaven, and the second is similar, as the Devil is presented as man's enemy. In other words, wearing no veil is a sign of weakness because women are allowing the Devil to lead them astray, while the question is meant to direct the viewer to the idea of nakedness.

as receiving approval from likeminded people through which women allegedly can earn heavenly rewards. They also largely believe that they are activists who resist mainstream ideas in their respective societies that either encourage women to be unveiled or wear traditional hijab. For niqabi salafist women, Islam remains a source of liberation because it elevates the status of women by regarding them as special, unique, and precious, and possibly more important than others, which entails a sense of supremacist ideology. In such a mindset, women must be well covered to be protected, as Islam can lead them to salvation and offer a path to heaven, whereas secular laws and a Westernized life can only distract them from becoming close to Allah (see the discussion below on the "Salafi Women" group), as both are part of the Western cultural hegemony and imperialism. Here, globalization and the West are being vigorously avoided, attacked, criticized, and confronted by those women along different facets of their lives. Some even attribute the "rise of religious rejuvenation," which emerged lately in some parts of the Middle East, as "a reaction against the West" (Fernea, 2010, p. xv) because Westernization and globalization are regarded by some as threats to traditional social values and destabilizing forces against the power of Islam and its practices. In fact, many of these salafi groups are closely affiliated with the ideology of the Muslim Brotherhood in Egypt and Wahabism in Saudi Arabia, especially with the ideas of Sayyid Qutb, the spiritual founder of Muslim Brotherhood. Qutb considered modern life as an extension of the *jahiliyyah* (pre-Islamic) era because Muslims are not observant of the orthodox teachings of Islam (Calvert, 2009; Khatab, 2006; Toth, 2013); hence, there is a need to return to the *salaf* (orthodox goodly forefathers) and imitate their way of life. With regard to women, they should largely emulate the practices of early Muslims, such as the wives of Prophet Muhammed, which includes wearing the niqab. Interestingly, the affordances of social media outlets, especially the anonymity they offer, have empowered niqabi women because they are no more geographically limited as well as confined to and hidden behind their black dresses; instead, they are as socially active as men, if not more, and can easily communicate with each other as well as to the wider general public by freely expressing political views without fear of punishment or physical harassment. Finally, one can identify a middle ground in Islamist feminism that is manifested in such online communities as "My Hijab is my Salvation" and "A Chaste Woman is Man's Treasure." For these Islamist feminists, Islam "gives women a sense of value and political purpose in these gendered roles and a sense of confidence as well," and "women are not less than men but equally important in different ways" (Karam, 1998, p. 22).

In the middle of the spectrum, we can also find what constitutes most of the mainstream culture in Arab countries such as Egypt, Iraq, Tunisia, and Morocco. Karam calls this category "Muslim feminism" (1997), as women identify with Islam and attempt to observe most of its moderate teachings by praying, fasting, and being good. The majority of these Muslim women wear the traditional veil, which they regard as an Islamic obligation toward Allah, who will reward them for being observant of basic religious teachings. In this category, Muslim feminists "are attempting to reconcile the discourses of Islam with human rights," and "their aim is to show that the discourse of total equality between men and women is Islamically valid" (Karam, 1997, p. 22). Unlike the niqabis, most hijabi women see no need in being too strict in following Islamic teachings, as the religion of Islam has given women rights and privileges that are not far different from what men have. As Mohammed El-Nawawy and Sahar Khamis observe, "Muslim feminists derive their power from their religion" (2009, p. 154). For such women, Islamic feminism is expected to "close gaps and reveal . . . common concerns and goals, starting with the basic affirmation of gender equality and social justice" (Badran, 2013, p. 246).

As stated above, this group constitutes the mainstream belief in many Muslim countries and includes moderate Muslims who believe in the equality of men and women (Carland, 2017) and in "conservatism and traditionalism," which after all provide "an appropriate alternative to radical Islam" (Schwartz, 2008, p. 235). In this context, only a minority of Muslim women living in countries such as Indonesia (12%), Iran (20%), and Turkey (18%) believe that their respective countries should adopt Western values on gender equality, while the majority believe that Islamic values must not be abandoned. For example, 81% of Iraqi women surveyed believe that "religious authorities should play a direct role in crafting family law" (Esposito & Mogahed, 2007, pp. 107, 113). Most importantly, Muslim women largely agree that they "deserve the same legal rights as men, to vote without influence from family members, to work at any job they are qualified for, and even to serve in the highest levels of government" (pp. 101–102). For example, 61% of Saudi women believe they should drive cars by themselves, and 69% that they should vote without any interference, while 76% believe they should work at any job they are qualified to do. As for Egyptian women, 88% of them believe they should work at any job for which they have the skills or experience (Esposito & Mogahed, 2007, p. 102). These women cite various religious texts that support their views on equality and women's rights, whereas the previous niqabi group also cites religious texts, but they do it to defend their views on the importance of following strict religious rules. In general, the majority of Muslim women "favor Islam's role in their lives, but they see a gap between the ideal and the Muslim world's reality," as other pressing issues such as "lack of unity, economic and political corruption, and extremism" seem to be far more important than the issue of gender equality (Esposito & Mogahed, 2007, p. 120). In this category, the ideas of Kuwaiti Muslim cleric Tarek Al Suwaidan are relevant, for on his TV show "Alamatny Al ḥay5401220103at" (Life Has Taught Me) on Al Resalah channel, he once spoke of "defin[ing] the rights of women in Islam, erasing misconceptions by practicing an Islamist feminist approach while reinterpreting the religious texts" (El Mkaouar, 2016).

Finally, and at the other end of the spectrum, Muslim feminists also include women who identify as secular, progressive, and/or liberal and do not necessarily wear the veil or follow all religious practices (Esack, 2003; Kurzman, 1998). This category includes some Sufi groups, whose women members

> affirm that Sufism allows them to maintain their Islamic identity in a personal and quietist way that does not draw them into the struggles with society that so many of their sister scholars are experiencing. They find in traditional mystical treatises and practices a way to transcend the mundane and to engage with the divine ion a level where all creatures are more or less equal and issues of gender equality do not need constantly to be argued. (Haddad, Smith & Moore, 2006, p. 160)

This type of feminism rejects the apparent submissiveness and passivity of some niqabi and veiled women; instead, these Muslim feminists believe in their agency and capability to create change in Islamic faith and to challenge religious authorities (Mandaville, 2001); for some of them, men and women can and should pray together in mosques, and women can issue fatwas (religious decrees) as well as lead prayers, such as the case of Amina Wadud, who became "the first woman to lead British Muslims in mixed congregational prayers and deliver the Friday sermon" (Butt & Nixon, 2008). Another example is women leading prayers and sitting with men in the Seyran Ateş's Ibn Rushd-Goethe mosque in Berlin (McGuinness, 2017; Oltermann, 2017). Here, Islam is more inclusive and regarded as a perpetual source of aesthetic beauty, strength, and spiritual elevation for women.

As discussed in Chapter 1, social media outlets are part of the online public sphere, and the concept of Ummah or Muslims' nation (Saunders, 2008) is relevant here, especially the online or virtual Ummah (Al-Rawi, 2015, 2017; Mandaville, 2001, 2003; Roy, 2004). Indeed, social media outlets provide users with the means to create a connective and collective identity that links them based on issues of gender, religion, ethnicity, age, race, activism, or other elements. In other words, the "distributive and networked technologies are helping Muslims to forge and sustain distanciated links reminiscent of the umma concept" (Mandaville, 2001, p. 190). Also, new media outlets provide empowerment tools for women in the Arab world to express personal views and reinterpret religious texts. Mandaville, for example, argues that the new Muslim figure is able to challenge authority including that of the mosque with the use of new media (2001, p. 190), while Akou observed in a study on Islamic hijab in online forums that many users are often involved in re-explaining religious teachings as a form of resistance against traditional religious authorities (2010). In his study of the blog Muslimah Media Watch, Nabil Echchaibi argues that this online platform functions as an alternative resistance outlet by "blending of texts as a rationale for their arguments and a frequent promotion of other Muslim women activists who have reinterpreted Qur'anic verses to privilege women's voices and challenge misogynist readings" (2013, p. 864). Similarly, Sahar Khamis provides different examples of the way satellite channels and new media outlets have offered new tools for activism and "self-expression and multiple resistances" against hegemonic perspectives against Muslim women (2010, p. 237).

Indeed, many women gather online to collectively create communities that can serve their own interests or agenda. The same applies to religious practices, for Muslim women from various religious affiliations, including salafists, sufis, shiites, secularists, and others, are often connected on certain platforms to express themselves, exchange views, be updated about relevant news, and/or show support for each other. In fact, a sense of sisterhood is created within the online community, as offline and online practices often merge (Campbell, 2012). These online practices are similar to what Muslims do in mosques, and Al-Rawi (2016) mentions how Facebook offers its users an online venue to express virtual collective prayers as well as religious beliefs, thoughts, and sentiments. In his study of the *Innocence of Muslims* film on Facebook, he found that many online users often post virtual prayers and supplications using language similar to that used offline and in a real mosque. In other words, Facebook functions as a virtual mosque.

In brief, many Muslim women are connected to each other online through sharing a Muslim female identity, while other religious factors can further bind them, such as political affiliations and geographical proximity. Here, social media platforms function as alternative media outlets, especially for people who have no way to express their views on mainstream media or other traditional channels. As will be shown in this chapter, some Muslim women's online communities such as the "Salafi Women" or "Niqabi yes, Complicated no" groups do not have formal venues other than social media outlets to collectively express their religious and political opinions. In addition, many members of the various online communities believe they are activists who can create change in their own societies. For instance, some Muslim feminist groups, such as those calling for women's equality and social justice, regard themselves as activists who try to resist traditional religious authorities and mainstream ideas, especially those coming from the West (see the discussion of "Muslim Women against Femen" in the upcoming section). In what follows, a discussion is presented on different Muslim women's online communities with a focus on their social media use.

Female Muslims Online Communities

There are hundreds, if not thousands, of Muslim women pages on social media, especially Facebook. Using the method I described in earlier chapters, I have selected the most popular ones in terms of the number of followers. As discussed above, online women's communities are situated along a spectrum, so the discussion below is structured based on the nature of religious beliefs and practices followed by each online group.

The first online community we will look at is found on the Facebook page "Women of Heaven" (نساء الجنة), which is the fifth most popular Facebook page in Egypt (see Table 3.1). This women's group promotes a moderate version of Islam by stressing the importance of women's modesty and faith in Muslims' lives. The page describes itself as an online publication that is "the leading luxury life style magazine for the Muslim Arab Women." Based on an examination of 140 collected images, the page's visuals relate primarily to general Islamic

Table 3.1. Social Networking Sites Cited in the Chapter

SNS	Followers/ views/ likes	Link
Women of Heaven	23.4m	www.facebook.com/nessaelgana
The Righteous Woman	682K	www.facebook.com/zawja1
Muslim Women against Femen	16K	www.facebook.com/MuslimWomenAgainstFemen
Princess by My Own Morals	2.3m	www.facebook.com/amirabakhlae
My Beautiful Beloved is a Muslim	842K	www.facebook.com/Habibaty.elgamila.muslima
My Veil is the Secret of My Beauty	13K	www.facebook.com 401865656542713-حجابي-هو-سر-جمالي
Muslim Girl	130K	www.facebook.com/muslimgirlarmy
Women of Paradise	1.6m	www.facebook.com/Paradise.Of.Women1
A Chaste Woman is Man's Treasure	3.4m	www.facebook.com/almar2a.al3afefah
My Hijab is my Salvation	156K	www.facebook.com/Hejaby
Niqabi yes, Complicated no!"	139K	www.facebook.com/ツ-ツ ツ-ツ-لا-منتقبه-اه-معقده ツ-ツ ツ-ツ ツ-181051345253723
Salafi Muslim Women	49K	www.facebook.com/musleimat.slafiat/?ref=br_rs
With My Niqab, I Satisfy My God	77K	www.facebook.com/myniqap
Niqabis	49K	www.facebook.com/mona9aba/?ref=br_rs
Niqabi and Proud of It	10K	www.facebook.com/-منقبة-و أفتخر 194887180521452/?ref=br_rsm
Virtuous Niqabis	12K	www.facebook.com/- منقبات-عفيفات 803373173117953/?ref=br_rs
Kingdom of Niqab	16K	www.facebook.com/kingdom.of.niqab

Data collected July 15, 2017.

prayers and supplications. Interestingly, many popular images imitate the Japanese anime style of big, colored eyes, white, round faces, small mouths, and other artistic features. This is probably due to the wish to provide a playful and somehow funny or "cool" aspect of hijabi women (see Figure 3.2). Most importantly, the images emphasize the importance of wearing the hijab, which allegedly can provide heavenly or worldly rewards for those who wear it. Another posted image conveys the message that wearing the veil presumably elevates women's status, making them "queens." The latter notion is similar to what some niqabi women's groups claim, as will be discussed below.[1]

A second moderate online community, "Muslim Women Against Femen," was created in 2013 to confront Femen, the popular feminist group well known for its topless protests and activism. Community members regard themselves as activists confronting cultural homogenization and Western imperialism by highlighting Islamic modesty and

Figure 3.2. Facebook page profile of "Women of Heaven."

faith instead of nakedness with an objective of emphasizing women's equality and freedom (Malkawi, 2013; Nelson, 2013). The community is linked to the Twitter hashtag movement #MuslimahPride, which has been used by many devout Muslim women to show their pride in Islam and describe how Islam has given them freedom and equality. The group contests the notion of female oppression and regards it as a justification by the West to interfere in Muslim women's lives and religious practices. This idea corresponds with the page's description:

> This page is for Muslim women who want to expose FEMEN for the Islamophobes/Imperialists that they are. We have had enough of Western feminists imposing their values on us. We are taking a stand to make our voices heard and reclaim our agency. Muslim women have had enough of this paternalistic and parasitic relationship with SOME Western feminists. The group is open to all, Muslim and non-Muslim, men and women. Peace.

In general, online engagement is limited, and most posts and comments are written in English, as the apparent targeted audience is largely Western. For example, the most liked post, which is also the most shared one, states the following: "This is how sisters in Berlin responded to Femen! #MuslimahPride." The post is meant to stress the oppositional disparity between Femen and Muslim Women against Femen movements, as it showcases a group of veiled women carrying signs that call for modesty in contrast to another group of topless women carrying signs that encourage nakedness. Incidentally, both women's groups share the notion of activism and resistance to assert their rights and freedoms, but they articulate it in completely different ways. The most commented-on post states: "Islam gave me freedom! From a sister in Brazil," which signifies the transnational nature of this small online community. (I should note that many other existing online Muslim women's groups are moderate in nature but cannot be discussed here because of space limitations. For the most part, these groups discuss ideas similar to the ones covered here.[2])

As already described, degrees of religious faith and practices are wide ranging, and other online women's communities appear to emphasize stricter rules than those found in the earlier examples of Muslim feminist communities. For instance, the online community of the Facebook page "A Chaste Woman is Man's Treasure" sounds much more conservative than those discussed thus far. The page's title suggests a clear misogynistic perception, as women are regarded as precious commodities that must be preserved and well kept, for they need to be veiled, young, and beautiful.[3] There is also no emphasis on women's empowerment, as the focus is on the importance of following religious rules and decrees. For example, many posts reference the teachings of the conservative Saudi preacher Muhammed Al-Arifi, as well as the Egyptian cleric Muhammed Al-Shaarawi, while one image showcases a well-veiled Muslim white woman with the adjoining text:

> A male's masculinity can be known by his wife's clothes when she goes out shopping. He who cannot overrule his wife when she faces other people cannot overrule her when he is with her at home. . . . There is behind every sensual woman walking in the streets a man who has lost his manhood and jealousy. . . . A woman without shyness is just a piece of meat walking amongst living beings.

Based on this statement—fairly typical among those found in online conservative or patriarchal cultures and communities—a woman's role in life is to be passive and weak, for her male partner must lead and guide her in every facet of her life.

A similar Islamist feminist online group is called "My Hijab is my Salvation." The name of this online community suggests women can earn salvation only by wearing the hijab and being religiously chaste—the two appear to be connected. For example, the Facebook page profile highlights a veiled woman without showing her face, stating: "Everything in life that is being taken care of enhances its beauty. A girl's chastity overpowers physical beauty and wealth." In other words, observing religious practices, particularly abstaining from extramarital sexual relationships, is more important than all else. Note that drawing faces and showing real images are regarded by many conservative and salafi groups as taboo or *haram* (religiously banned), which might explain why the woman in the Facebook profile has no face (Baljon, 1994).

According to its self-description, the objective of this online community is "assisting Muslim sisters in observing the legitimate hijab and succeeding in different facets of life. . . . My goal is to remove any misunderstanding and misconceptions about the legitimate Islamic

Hijab . . . hoping that the platform allows free exchange of ideas, experiences, and debates among the sisters who observe the legitimate hijab." "Legitimate hijab" suggests that the traditional hijab might not be religiously sufficient, so some Muslim women should wear another layer, such as an *abayya* (full-length gown or garment that is usually black) to better cover themselves. Similar to the Facebook page profile, many of the posted images do not show women's faces; for example, one image includes a message in English regarding the "proper" or "legitimate" way to wear the veil, as it is supposed to cover the features of women's bodies rather than only "wrapping" the body with clothes. This is, of course, a rather strict view of how to wear the veil, a view not advocated by communities discussed earlier.

On the other end of this spectrum, we find the niqabi women's online communities that call for wearing the niqab and strictly observing Islamic practices to create a sense of sisterhood around the niqab-wearing practice. They regard themselves as activists whose mission is to preach the perceived heavenly and worldly rewards of wearing the niqab to anyone interested. Among these communities is "Niqabi yes, Complicated no!," an Egyptian group that is part of the salafist "Network towards Allah." Here is a passage from the community's self-description:

> To all Muslim girls. . . . By Allah's will, our goal is to see all girls act like the faithful wives of Prophet Muhammed with their veils and morals. This is based on the notion that the niqabi woman is not reclusive, complicated, pessimistic, depressed, ugly, neglectful, and sad all the time. She is also not a terrorist and is not concealing anything bad with the niqab and does not have a black heart. All of this is related to old fashioned way of thinking which is weird and irrational. The niqabi woman is a very normal person who eats, drinks, and feels happy and sad [similar to other people]. She goes to college to learn and does not like to be depressed or to complicate matters. She has not buried herself in life. But the whole idea [behind the niqab] is that her love for God has filled her heart, and she views herself as very precious; hence, she wears a dress that can protect her, for she is a jewel, and Jewels cannot be viewed by everyone. . . . Proud of my Niqab.

This description reveals that many niqabi women face prejudice and stereotypical views held against them, especially associating them with terrorism and political violence. With regard to the Facebook page's analysis, most images and posts emphasize following a strict version of Islam, with a focus on the pride of wearing the niqab. See, for example, Figure 3.3, which shows a clear usage of the Japanese anime style, highlighting that wearing the niqab is evidence of fully obeying Allah's decrees. The text reads: "Proud of my niqab. Niqab wearing is not regressive and backward and does not limit freedom. Instead, it is part of Allah's blessing, grace, and obedience from which we come closer to the Almighty." The implicit message of this online community is that the traditional hijab is not fully "legitimate," and that the niqab (legitimate hijab) is the "true" solution for Muslim women's faith and salvation as a way to prove their obedience and subjection to God. Interestingly, "legitimate hijab" appears to be defined and applied differently here from in our first example above, relative to the religious beliefs and values of each online community. Hanna Papanek, for example, observed that Pakistani women who wore the burqa regarded it as a "portable seclusion" device, as it liberates them from the confines of segregated spaces inside their homes (as cited in Abu-Lughod, 2002).

Figure 3.3. Two images from "Niqabi yes, Complicated no!" Facebook page.

Another image retrieved from the community's Facebook page provides further details on the "legitimate hijab," which includes observing seven strict conditions: the hijab (1) should cover the entire body; (2) should not resemble men's clothes or that of "infidel" women; (3) should be wide and not tight; (4) should not be scented; (5) should not be transparent; (6) should not have decorations on it; and (7) should not be worn for fame. The phrase "infidel" women here could be a reference to unveiled or Western women, and in contrast to the previous online communities, this group refers to "infidel women" several times in its online chatter, which is one way of asserting their perceived superiority. In brief, this online community views the niqab as empowerment because it is understood as a tool that elevates women to a higher and unique status in the way it allegedly dignifies and protects women. Also, the concept of freedom as interpreted by the niqabi women community is different from that of the mainstream. Most members of this online community regard themselves as activists who resist the cultural imperialism, globalization, secularism, and liberalism associated with Western hegemony, corruption, and apostasy. Unlike the other online communities that call for women's freedom, this online group does not refer to women's equality, sexuality, and rights, as these arguments and references are largely absent from the online debates. For instance, the concept of freedom is defined as the willingness to practice religion freely, especially wearing the niqab, rather than focusing on personal choices and liberties. One image, for example, reads, "Niqab entails freedom. Liberalism, do you understand!," whereas another showcases a niqabi woman whose face is not shown and reads, "Pardon me, this is the freedom that we seek." In other words, freedom is limited to the act of wearing the niqab, following strict rules of Islam, and obeying Allah's other decrees. Indeed, this is an unorthodox definition of the value of freedom, as it touches on the principle of freedom of religious practice and belief. It is also not associated with the traditional concept of liberal thought and behavior because "freedom" for niqabis entails strictly following Allah's orders. Paradoxically, though, the members of the niqabi woman's community regard following man or Allah's rules as freedom of religion despite the fact that they have no agency or will to personally choose and change some of these practices that are dictated by others.

Similar to the "Niqabi yes, Complicated no!" community is the "Salafi Women" group. But a major difference distinguishes the two, as the latter group is more ideologically oriented, with most members regarding themselves as political activists. The group's Facebook page reads as follows: "Who am I? I'm a salafi Muslim. Neither a terrorist nor regressive. Allah and His Prophet's love is an essential need. My path is Allah's book, the Prophet's life, and understanding the [wisdom] of his good companions. I neither develop [different or new religious principles] nor disobey my Prophet. . . . We'll live with dignity." As can be seen, salvation for salafi women lays in strictly following religious rules and refraining from questioning any aspect of Islamic religion as long as it is produced by "authentic" religious circles. Similar to groups we have looked at previously, this online community employs a Japanese anime style (which can be seen in their Facebook page profile). At the bottom of its Facebook banner has been added the term "Hazimyat," which means "firm" or "steadfast," but it can also refer to followers of Hazim Salah Abu Islmael, the imprisoned Muslim Brotherhood leader.

This group appears to be more aggressive and assertive than "Niqabi yes, Complicated no!" in highlighting alleged injustices against niqabi women in Muslim societies, as many of its members regard themselves as activists whose mission is focused on voicing niqabi women's concerns and achieving more rights for them. For example, one post relates to niqabi women's rights in Egypt, claiming they have been greatly wronged, especially after Abdel Fattah El-Sisi's military takeover. The post reads: "Isn't it part of women's rights to avoid embarrassment, insult, and being expelled from the Armed Forces Club for wearing the niqab? In some places, she is treated similar to a dog, for you can see an announcement in front of the Club stating that niqabis and dogs are not allowed entry???? Are women's rights related to nakedness only?" The passage refers to an incident involving a niqabi woman in Egypt who was prevented from entering the Armed Forces Club. In general, there is a clear political orientation in this online community, with many graphic photos of injured and murdered protesters from the Egyptian Muslim Brothers (EMB). Its members are sympathetic to and supportive of EMB's followers and leaders such as Muhammed Morsi and Hazim Abu Ismael. Another post is a press release issued by Ansar Bait Al-Maqdis, an Egyptian terrorist group affiliated with ISIS, in which the group vows to attack the gas pipeline that extends from Egypt to Jordan. Other posts support Jabhat Al-Nusra, a terrorist Syrian group once affiliated with Al-Qaeda. Dozens of similar niqabi online communities are accessible across social media platforms.[4]

Our analysis indicates that the various communities formed online are quite segregated from each other based on religious devotion and beliefs. The online community of "Niqabi yes, Complicated no!," for example, is not associated at all with more moderate or liberal Muslim communities, and vice versa.

To conclude, despite the abundance of online Muslim women's communities, there are clear patterns by which they can be categorized, as groups have different degrees of religious observance and lack thereof. These online groups are regarded as extensions of their offline religious practices since social media outlets assist them in disseminating their values, enhancing their networks, and voicing their concerns. The online public sphere offered by Facebook and other social media outlets is clearly divided along ideological lines, as each online group is situated within a bubble of likeminded people and communities. Many members of these online communities are religious activists vigorously promoting their values and beliefs.

Chapter 4

Political Activism and Social Movements

This chapter deals with the way social media outlets provide an important venue for political activism by expressing Arab women's grievances and concerns. I argue that the Arab Spring events empowered women to be more vocal and assertive in demanding political rights and equality with men. Activists managed to express their dissatisfaction with the social and political reality on the ground, such as lack of employment opportunities, corruption, and inequality (Al-Rawi, 2014). This chapter examines popular online protests on social media such as Facebook and Twitter that championed women's causes in the Arab world, especially women's equality with men and freedom to express their political views without fear of being targeted or harmed. These online movements, organized by Arab women who challenged moral codes, stereotypes, and old customs, are never confined to specific countries as they serve to unite many Arab women and men from different regions, forming collective identity and action.

In a culture characterized by its patriarchal nature, as explained in Chapter 1, women find it difficult to assert their political demands and achieve equal rights with men in the Arab world. According to Hofstede's cultural dimensions theory, most Arab countries are high in masculinity and low in femininity (Hofstede, 1998; Hofstede & Hofstede, 2001; Hofstede, Hofstede, & Minkov, 1991) which partly explains the patriarchal nature of these societies. It is important to note that this phenomenon also extends to Western states in varying degrees. For example, West and Blumberg assert that taken-for-granted laws and cultural gender codes influence the way women participate in political activism that "has been socially constructed, or, more accurately male constructed" (West & Blumberg, 1991, p.4). In the Arab context, it is relevant to refer to feminist postcolonial theory. Radha Hegde, Gayatri Spivak, and Raka Shome discuss the concept of subalternity, which emphasizes women's lack of representation in the public sphere. When there are various kinds of repression in the political system, women's voices are not heard (Spitzack & Carter, 1987), as those in the male-dominated powerful elite become unresponsive to women's rights and demands; after all, women are viewed as too weak to have an influence in politics, so they are not taken seriously.

As described in Chapter 1, new technologies such as social media have assisted in creating a global networked society (Castells, 2012) that connects people interested in activist causes (Winder, 2014, p. 4). This is because the internet has been an effective platform for activism (Chadwick & Howard 2009), and social networking sites in particular have attracted more people worldwide to join in public debates on diverse political or societal issues due to the affordances they present. Segerberg and Bennet (2011) and many others argue that social media has become a key tool in political activism. Part of the popularity of social media channels stems from ordinary citizens' frustration with "social control and manipulation by powerful political, corporate and media forces" (Keren, 2006, 149). Another factor is the exclusion of many groups from mainstream media channels, as discussed earlier, so they naturally resort to social networking sites to freely express their views and organize their movement (Bennett, 2003; Carroll & Hackett, 2006; Kahn & Kellner, 2004). Arab female activists particularly do not appear to have proper platforms to address sensitive issues related to their daily lives. Social networking sites have thus become their preferred medium, functioning as alternative media channels (Chang, 2005). The so-called "networked public sphere" coined by Yochai Benkler (2006) appears to fit well in the feminist movement, as women and men are connected by social media channels to exchange political views and work as watchdogs to monitor their societies. Indeed, social networking sites constitute the very fabric of the public sphere by enhancing deliberative democracy and social contention, though the bonds that link protestors and activists do not last long (Burgess & Green, 2009, p. 77; Calhoun, 2004). However, this online public sphere does not mean that the virtual feminist community as a whole is present there;

instead, it is largely divided among separate online communities in what is termed the "public sphericules" (Gitlin, 1998), a concept indicating that there is no ideal single public sphere, as Habermas envisioned—instead there are multiple and often antagonistic public spheres (Cunningham et al., 2000).

Another relevant concept that needs to be elaborated here is hashtag activism in connection to feminist issues. Popular and trending hashtags like #BringBackOurGirls, #YesAllWomen, #HeForShe, #MeToo, and #StandWithWendy have garnered the attention of millions of Twitter users (Chittal, 2015). In the Arab world, hashtags like #Expose a harasser (#أفضح متحرش) allow women to film and take photos of sexual harassment to publicly shame the perpetrators. This hashtag became particularly popular in Egypt and elsewhere in the Arab world. Also, Facebook and blogging allow Muslim women in Morocco and Saudi Arabia to discuss a variety of issues, including "their personal legal status, discourses on feminism, redefining gender roles, sexuality . . . [as] these platforms are useful not only for coalescing around key social and political issues pertaining to women, but also for initiating social change" (Khannous, 2011, p. 358). In this chapter, five feminist movements are investigated. The selection of these movements is based on their local and regional popularity.

Political Activism and Social Movements

Social movements are broadly defined, ranging from the drive of a well-funded political party to chaotic, unorganized demands for change with plenty of zeal but no specified goals (Freeman & Johnson, 1999). Some scholars regard social movements as "collective organized actions to bring about or resist change by means of various historically conditioned strategies" (West & Blumberg 1991, p. 4; Tilly 1978). These social movements seek to form collective identity, as their members are "involved in conflictual relations with clearly identified opponents; are linked by dense informal networks; [and] share a distinct collective identity" (Della Porta & Diani, 2006, p. 20). They often emerge as a reaction against repressive conditions in a political or social system, and they aim at mobilizing the public around a goal to create a favorable change (Tilly, 1978; Zald & McCarthy, 1987). Snow and colleagues

(2008) further clarify that "collectivities give voice to their grievances and concerns about the rights, welfare, and well-being of themselves and others engaging in various types of collective action, such as protesting in the streets, that dramatize those grievances and concerns and demand that something be done about them" (p. 3). Yuce, Agarwal, Wigand, Lim, and Robinson (2014) studied the online collective action of the Oct26driving campaign by analyzing the diffusion of hashtags. Due to hacking and shutting down the campaign's website on October 9, 2013, hashtags spread virally and "contributed toward consolidating the web traffic to other social media platforms, primarily Twitter" (p. 408). By examining 70,000 tweets from 116 countries, the authors found interconnected collective actions, such as those related to women's rights.

For a social movement to succeed, social activists must make use of the available resources around them, which is linked to discussion on resource mobilization theory (Jenkins, 1981). This is accomplished through relying on social networking channels and reducing the time and effort invested on resources that cannot be attained, such as access to mainstream media channels, state funding, or massive social support. Making use of new technologies, many groups organize online due to the speed, ease, and relative freedom, creating what is called "pressure from below" that can circumvent traditional hierarchies of power (Juris 2005, p. 341). McAdam and colleagues (1996) confirm that social movements need three components to emerge and develop: mobilizing structures, opportunity structures, and framing processes. Mobilizing structures refer to the mechanisms that allow activists to organize themselves and be involved in social action (McAdam et al. 2001). Social networking sites play a major role here. Opportunity structures denote the importance of the context or circumstances in creating a social movement, while framing processes, which refer to the way social movement organizers use culturally shared values, assist in presenting, discussing, and framing the activists' cause in a way that creates a desirable impact (McAdam et al., 2001). Based on this hypothesis, I argue that the feminist movements discussed in this chapter would not have successfully emerged or flourished if the Arab Spring events had not occurred, as the latter paved the way and provided favorable political circumstances for the former. The same argument applies to the proliferation of new technologies that are regarded as vital resources for activism.[1]

Women's Activism in the Arab World

The first two social movements explored here relate to Saudi women's activist efforts to drive cars. For a variety of cultural reasons, Saudi Arabia used to be among the few places in the world where women were not allowed to drive. In fact, there was no civil law that prohibited women from driving in Saudi Arabia, but there were fatwas, which people generally observed in this highly conservative Muslim society. King Salman of Saudi Arabia lifted the driving ban for women in late September 2017, as well as another ban on attending football matches, in January 2018. These were regarded as positive steps toward emancipation and equality for women (BBC News, 2017c; Duerden, 2018). However, the real goal of these new policies was to promote to the outside world the idea that Saudi Arabia was implementing social and liberal reforms, which occurred partly because of increasing international pressure. For example, the Saudi government spent money to create political advertisements and air them on British TV channels to brand Saudi Arabia as a progressive country (Waterson, 2018). However, soon afterward, the Saudi government arrested prominent female activists, including Loujain al-Hathloul (discussed below), and allegedly tortured them (Amos, 2018).

The #Women2Drive movement, led by Saudi female activist Manal Al-Sharif, began in April 2011 and continued into 2013 (see Table 4.1 on page 58) (Agarwal et al., 2015; Ahmari, 2013). Al-Sharif claims to be the first female Saudi information security analyst and an ethical hacker; with colleagues, she created a Facebook campaign called "Teach Me How to Drive So I Can Protect Myself," as well as another called "Women to drive." In May 2011, al-Sharif was filmed by Wajiha al-Huwaider driving her car in Khobar city, and the 8-minute video was posted on YouTube (Al-Rasheed, 2013, p. 63). Al-Sharif was later charged for "disturbing public order . . . by twice driving in a bid to press her cause" (Macfarquhar, 2011). She was sentenced to 10 lashes for driving, though this sentence was later overturned and Al-Sharif and her colleagues were released (Alahmed, 2014; Associated Press, 2014). The campaign succeeded in drawing international attention to the cause of women's driving (Al-Rasheed, 2013; Chaudhry, 2014). Al-Sharif later published a book, *Daring to Drive* (2017), to describe her experiences. Yet she decided to quit social media in 2018 as a protest against the

Table 4.1. Social Networking Sites Cited in the Chapter

SNS	Likes/ views/ followers	Link
Manal Al-Sharif	298K	twitter.com/manal_alsharif
Women to Drive	37K	www.facebook.com/Saudi-Women-To-Drive-227817097234537
SaudiWomen2Drive	1.2m	www.youtube.com/user/SaudiWomen2Drive
No Woman, No Drive	14.4m	www.youtube.com/watch?v=aZMbTFNp4wI
Oct26Driving	23.8K	twitter.com/oct26driving
Oct26Driving	4.9m	www.youtube.com/user/oct26driving
Oct26Driving	10K	www.instagram.com/oct26driving
Loujain al-Hathloul	291K	twitter.com/LoujainHathloul
Maysa al-Amoudi	202K	twitter.com/maysaaX
Uprising of Women in the Arab World	120K	www.facebook.com/intifadat.almar2a
Revolution against Patriarchal Society	59K	www.facebook.com/Revolution.on.the.males.society
Girls' Revolution	145K	www.facebook.com/EgyGirlsRev

Data collected July 13, 2017.

flaming and trolling she received, stating: "Twitter now is becoming a trap, and it's being used in a very efficient way by those governments, dictatorships and tyrants to silence us, and not only that, to spread their own propaganda, their own hate speech, misinformation and disinformation" (Graham-Harrison, 2018). In this case, social media has become a negative tool employed by certain regimes and actors in surveillance, spying, and oppression, and many social media platforms are complicit in these efforts for not taking the necessary and prompt action for prevention (Noble, 2018).

Regarding the Saudi2Drive social media campaign, the top ten most-liked Facebook posts are examined because they provide an indication on the audience engagement with the campaign. Incidentally, all the top posts are written in English rather than Arabic, which indicates the kind of global support the movement's organizers garner and seek. This is closely connected to the influence of globalization and the interconnected collective action that some social movements attempt to achieve (Winder, 2014; Yuce, Agarwal, Wigand, Lim, & Robinson, 2014). In this regard, social and mainstream media are used to raise awareness about the campaign, as some of the top posts contain links to multiple platforms, such as newspaper articles and YouTube videos that deal with the movement's main cause, and all the top posts concern women's issues, proclaiming pride in the Saudi women's achievements or demanding more political rights in different fronts. An emphasis appears to be on opinion leaders, as Manal Al-Sharif, the most prominent figure in this movement, is highlighted in one of the posts.

Oct26driving, the second Saudi movement we will examine here, started in October 2013, mostly through the efforts of two Saudi women: Loujain al-Hathloul and Maysa al-Amoudi. Both women had online and offline influence long before their involvement in this movement. al-Hathloul was a famous Saudi vlogger who posted popular short videos on Keek about her experience living as a university student in Canada without wearing a veil. Her vlogs created controversy because she tried to break cultural taboos regarding what Saudi women should say and whether they should post public videos detailing their personal experiences. This connects to the way the diffusion of innovation occurs, especially through the aid of opinion leaders (Rogers, 2010). Similarly, al-Amoudi is a well-known Saudi journalist based in the UAE. On November 30, 2014, al-Hathloul tried to drive her car to cross the Saudi border using her Emirati driving license, but she was stopped and her passport confiscated (Mackey, 2015). al-Amoudi headed toward al-Hathloul from the UAE to provide her with food and support, but both were arrested on the following day (Associated Press, 2014). Since neither woman had literally broken Saudi law, there was no other jurisdiction to try them except in terrorism court under the pretense that they had incited "public disorder" (Bager, 2015). To show support of the Saudi authorities, the UAE issued a decree to prevent Loujan al-Hathloul from returning, and on December 10, 2015, she was arrested and held for about 70 days before her release in February 2016 (Chaudhry, 2014). al-Hathloul received ample public support for her movement to end the ban on women driving and the male guardianship system; this support came from many sides, including Saudi men. For example, to connect with the movement, Hisham Fageeh performed a song he called "No Woman, No Drive," an adaptation of a Bob Marley song. Fageeh's friend Fahad Albutairi later married al-Hathloul, citing their common interest in women's activism (O'Grady, 2015). As I write this, Al-Hathloul has again been arrested by Saudi authorities for her activism and has allegedly been tortured and sexually harassed (Stancati & Said, 2018).

Many conservative voices in the Saudi Kingdom were critical of the Oct26driving movement and expressed great opposition to it. Saudi preacher Abu Zaid Al-Saidi, for example, tweeted an embedded threat on September 22, 2013: "If some slut women happen to drive on this day, then I expect some young reckless male drivers [Dirbaoyiah] to do what is required #Oct26driving." Al-Saidi was obviously encouraging young men to harass women if they attempted to drive. On June 4, 2017, al-Hathloul was arrested again at King Fahad International Airport in Dammam upon her return from Bahrain, with no reason given for her arrest (Amnesty International, 2017; Mortimer, 2017). The goal, of course, was to discourage her future travels and silence her in indirect ways, while hashtags such as "You won't drive, won't drive" (#لن تقودي، لن تقودي) started trending in Saudi Arabia as a way of rejecting the idea of allowing women to drive cars.

Though there is no Facebook page and its website (www.oct26driving.com) is no longer in operation because it was hacked (Yuce, Agarwal, Wigand, Lim, & Robinson, 2014), an interesting element about the Oct26driving movement is its Instagram page, which contains primarily selfies taken by Saudi women while driving or others showing them holding driving licenses issued in other countries. Some of the more common hashtags that accompany the Instagram posts are "Driving_alone," "Loujain_on_the_border," "women_driving," "Loujain_thelionhearted," and "trial_of_Loujain_and_Maysaa." The movement organizer's motto is "Women's driving is a choice not enforcement," and the campaign stresses six areas that could demonstrate support for the movement: sending a picture or video of a Saudi woman driving, posting an image or drawing that shows support, sending a video or audio clip that expresses support, expressing support on Twitter by using the hashtag #Oct26driving, participating in public debates on mainstream media like TV and radio channels to speak about the campaign, and placing the campaign's logo on someone's car or in a public place. In short, multiplatform activism is implemented by employing offline and online techniques, while social media assisted in spreading information and raising awareness. Aside from using a Gmail account, the campaign organizers' urge their followers to contact them using the mobile phone application WhatsApp to ensure privacy and protection.

As for the social media campaign, the online interaction that occurs on the movement's Twitter account is explored through the Twitter outlets of Loujain al-Hathloul and Maysa al-Amoudi.[2] Regarding Maysa al-Amoudi's Twitter account, the Saudi activist describes herself as "Femminista, Presenter-journalist from Mecca," and her profile picture shows her removing her hijab to show her hair, which can be interpreted as an act of rebellion against cultural taboos in Saudi Arabia or liberation from these norms. The third most-retweeted post was on November 30, 2014, stating: "I've just met with Loujain Hathloul on the border. The guards want my ID and refuse that I cross. I've only come to support and do not insist on crossing the border #Loujain-lion-hearted." The high number of retweets shows the followers' engagement with the Oct26driving movement. Loujain Al-Hathloul's Twitter page shows a woman with the message "I'm responsible for my own affairs," while Al-Hathloul is shown without a veil, similar to Al-Amoudi's page. In examining the top 10 most-retweeted posts that received the highest amount of engagement, we find that only two posts were not related to the Oct26driving campaign, while all the remaining ones were focused on the movement, indicating Al-Hathloul's dedication to the cause and the public's interest in this movement.

The main Twitter page of the Oct26driving campaign has photos of Al-Hathloul and Al-Amoudi as its profile image. In fact, six of the top 10 most-retweeted posts deal with Al-Hathloul and Al-Amoudi, showing their central roles in the movement, while the remaining four posts are more general about the movement and how to support it. Most of the online chatter is focused on these two figures. In general, the majority of the most active users are Saudi female activists who are less well known than Al-Hathloul and Al-Amoudi, while there are also a Saudi NGO and Al-Jazeera English correspondent in the top 10 most active users' list. Indeed, this closely relates to the kind of interconnected collective action often required to form a social movement. In terms of the role of globalization and international cooperation with the movement, the majority of online engagement comes from Saudi Arabia, with two non-Arab countries (the United States and Turkey) ranking second and third.

It is important to mention here that many social movements are hierarchical in nature, as there is a clear centralization in the discussion and attention given to some leading figures. In the case of the Oct26driving movement, al-Hathloul and Al-Amoudi are the focal points and opinion leaders since most online engagement centers on them. This is also manifested in the Twitter image profile used by the movement. It appears that the two figures have made use of their previous online and offline fame to attract more attention to their cause, which is typical of the way opinion leaders garner support and raise awareness (Katz, 1957; Katz & Lazarsfeld, 1955). In fact, the Twitter followers of al-Hathloul and Al-Amoudi number over 477,000, though, as of November 2016, the movement itself has only 24,358 followers. As discussed in Chapter 2, opinion leaders or influentials are needed in some movements to exert influence in their own environments. This has possibly been enhanced due to the cultural taboos surrounding women. In the case of the Oct26driving campaign, it appears that the previous liberal political views of al-Hathloul and Al-Amoudi have helped them garner support from a wide variety of Saudis, and their ideas have now expanded beyond the demand for the right to drive to include calls for greater autonomy and independence for women living in a highly masculine and patriarchal culture. These activism efforts are meant to encourage more people to be vocal and demand rights, and indications are that awareness regarding women's rights and equality in Saudi Arabia is on the upswing.[3]

The third movement we will look at is "Uprising of Women in the Arab World," which was created by four Arab women—Yalda Younes, Diala Haidar, Farah Barqawi, and Sally Zohney—living in different countries, creating a network of activists using Facebook, Flikr, and Twitter. The movement's organizers and followers believe in political equality between men and women, freedom of speech, and women's independence, and its slogan is "Together for free, independent and fearless women in the Arab world" (Uprising of Women in the Arab World, 2011b). Thousands of photos have been uploaded by activists featuring Arab and Western women carrying signs centering on the issue of equality and justice for women.

An analysis of the 70,483 commentators on the movement's Facebook page reveals that 62% (44,016) are females and 37% (26,467) are males. Although female commentators outnumber males, some of the males are involved in these new women's movements for various motives, including their desire to back women up. Such support also appears in the discussion of Oct26driving, and by Sally Zohney, who referred to the kind of support her Facebook page often receives: "It's not just the two or three friends we know, or the network we personally have. It's men . . . from countries like Saudi Arabia where we didn't expect support" (Abbas, 2012).

The movement's Facebook page includes many posts in English, denoting its global outreach. For example, the movement calls for a global stance against what they term "sexual terrorism" against women as practiced in many Arab countries, especially Egypt. Women activists from the United States posted pictures of their protests in front of Egyptian embassies and made comments to reject the way Egyptian women protesters were treated in the streets. In one of the posts, the Facebook organizers called on Arab women to "rebel against the symbols of repression and control, to rebel against what is called the veil that man imposes on you, to rebel against the niqab that man forces you to wear like a halter." The poster affirms that Islam originally came to uplift Arabs from the regression of polytheism and never forced women to wear the veil.

As for the most frequent comments made by the public highlighted in Al-Rawi's study (2014), we find that "Saudi Arabia" (in English) is a recurrent phrase, which is to be expected in light of the preoccupation, especially in the West, with the issues of women's rights in Saudi Arabia (e.g., women drivers, voting, interacting with male strangers in public). As for the term "Muslim women" (in English), several comparisons are made with "Western women" liberties and freedoms. According to Tucker, "gender segregation and/or female seclusion and veiling, and strict rules and sanctions for sexual behavior are the hot topics of the day" in Western media discourse (2008, p. 175). Further, Abu-Lughod and El-Mahdi assert that "Orientalist understandings of Arab and Muslim women" shape the way Westerners view Arab women (2011, p. 683). In short, there appear to be some preconceived perceptions that blame Islam rather than the way some Islamic teachings are (mis)interpreted or old cultural beliefs to be behind the degradation of women's status. In this regard, commentators appear to generally agree that Arab women's lack of freedom is not caused by Islam itself; instead, some religious men and/or "traditions and customs" are to blame. For example, one female commentator, Sahar Ghanem, discussed the issue of wearing the veil, stating it is a personal choice, as neither religious men nor anyone "else has the right to impose certain dress codes on others not even in the name of religion" because it is not clearly stated in the Quran. Such comments are supported by the organizers of the Facebook page. For example, Sally Zohney reveals that one of the major issues that they encounter is "the abuse of the religious discourse. We are conservative by nature [in Egypt] and we tend not to argue when it comes to religion. Where people are illiterate, the imam knows best" (Stewart 2013). On the other hand, another female commentator, Zahrat Al-Madain, asserted that women's backward condition in the Arab world is caused by "refraining from adhering to religion" and that the "uprising must be directed against those who pretend to be religious to humiliate women in the name of religion while [Islam] is far from this." The discussion above on the role of religion in society is one example of Gitlin's public sphericules since there are different groups of commentators, each with his or her own stance toward the same issue.

Finally, the movement's Facebook often disseminates images taken and used in other women's campaigns in the region, which indicates solidarity and coordination among women's movements and their interconnected collective action. The majority of images show a woman carrying a statement that contains the message to be communicated, and most of the women's faces are shown, which indicates that the majority feel proud and empowered in revealing their true identities to the online public. Issues relate primarily to women's protection in society, equal legal and political rights with men, rejecting the rape culture, and street and sexual harassment. Regional solidarity is also stressed; one image, for instance, communicates a general statement of support: "I'm with the 'Uprising of women in the Arab world' [movement] because I'm responsible for myself." Incidentally, the latter image was also used by Al-Hathloul on her Twitter page after removing "Uprising of women in the Arab world." Indeed, the movement attracts women from different parts of the Arab world because they share a collective political goal, and many have mutual concerns and suffer from similar problems and issues.

The fourth movement to be examined here is the "Girls' Revolution," created on January 25, 2012. Its Facebook page was created by a young Egyptian girl, Ghadeer Ahmed, who first appeared in her promo video on May 8, 2012, in a veil, but the following video clip on July 1, 2012, showed her without one (Girls' Revolution, 2012b, 2012c). On its Facebook page, the movement is described as a "Revolution against anything that is backward. I'm a girl; I'm human; I'm free" (Girls' Revolution, 2012a).

Again based on Al-Rawi's study (2014), an analysis of the 61,267 commentators interacting on the movement's Facebook page reveals that 59% (36,336) are females and 40% (24,931) are males. Some of the main issues discussed on this page relate to women's freedom and rights. One post mentions how dissenting voices are silenced: "Every time we discuss women's freedom, we start reading comments suggesting that we seek immorality. Blasphemy about women's freedom is similar to blasphemy about women's education." Hundreds of commentators oppose the idea that women should stop wearing the veil. Focus on what women should or should not wear is apparent, many posts stating that the dress code must be strictly followed. For example, one of the most frequent phrases is "hijab is a religious obligation," followed by "the martyred Imam Hasan Al-Banna," who is the founder of the Muslim Brotherhood movement; most of these posts relate to pictures of women shown without a veil. Posting Al-Banna's reference or picture is one way of showing the hardline religious view of the Facebook poster who regards any calls for women's freedom or removing their veils to be against the basic framework of Islam. One female commentator said, for instance: "Wearing the veil is without doubt a religious obligation. . . . Women are beautiful creatures and were ordered to wear the veil because they naturally seduce men. . . . Besides, wearing the veil makes women look more beautiful, dignified, and reserved." Another female commentator believes that women's freedom must be linked to the freedom of wearing the veil and niqab, "which is a sign of women's freedom in choosing her dress and finding her own way of thinking." Discussions on sexual harassment are recurrent, some of which cite the veil as a means to deter harassment, while another states that the "hijab is a religious obligation." Discussions often become heated between opponents and supporters of wearing the veil.

The last movement we will look at in this chapter is "Revolution against Patriarchal Society," formed by a 20-year-old Iraqi girl, Ruqaya Abidalli. Its Facebook page was created on September 7, 2012. According to its organizer, the movement is meant to be a protest against "the demeaning view on women" (Al-Sarai, 2012) in some Arab societies. The Facebook page calls on women to: "Revolt on history and achieve victory on the major illusion . . . since the sun is the graveyard of falcons. Revolt on an East that views you as a feast on its bed" (Revolution against Patriarchal Society, 2012). The banner appearing on the movement's Facebook page contains a quotation from well-known Arab feminist writer Ghada Al-Samman, who is allegedly quoted as saying: "Arabs do not agree on anything but on their backward attitude toward women." The Facebook page also describes the expected revolution as a "radical" one that is needed to "destabilize the unjust and old traditions and customs" (Revolution against Patriarchal Society, 2012). We find that commentators make many references to famous Arab feminist writers, such as Al-Samman, Nawal Al-Saadawi, and Syrian poet Nazar Qabani, who is well known for attacking traditional social and political practices that limit women's freedom (see chapter 4).

In his study, Al-Rawi (2014) examined gender distribution among the 22,878 commentators on the movement's Facebook page, revealing that 64% (14,763) were female and 35% (8,115) were male, indicating feminist interest in this movement. Further, the analysis of these comments indicates that "violence against women" is one of the main topics discussed by posters (Al-Rawi, 2014), and this issue is highly connected with one of the most recurrent terms "customs and traditions" (العادات و التقاليد), indicating that cultural beliefs rather than religious convictions are behind this social problem.

In the posts, the term "Eastern man" has negative connotations, as it is highly associated with "woman's body"; there is also a great deal of discussion on either rejecting or agreeing on the importance of the dress code, such as wearing wide, flowing dresses or even the veil to avoid sexual harassment. Similar to content on the Facebook page of the "Girls' Revolution," movement, direct criticism is aimed at religious men, who are also called "merchants of religion" because they are framed as profiteers with their *fatwas* (e.g., see Riemersma & van Tol, 2010). To give one example of these critical statements, the Facebook organizer posted the following: "religious men banned newspapers when they were first published . . . banned schools when they first started . . . afterwards they changed their minds and permitted them, so you find the one who banned attending schools sending his son to them and the one who banned using telephone to use it himself."

More importantly, the majority of commentators stand against the claim made by religious men that women "lack reason and faith" (العادات و التقاليد). The Facebook organizer stated in another post that such a claim is frequently repeated by "ignorant sheikhs and Wahhabi extremists and are only echoed by backward people." The poster cites examples from history on how women can excel and achieve greater success than men in science and politics and attributes this claim to "repressed and unsuccessful men who suffer complexes due to their ignorance and failure." The idea that women lack reason and faith is based on an Islamic belief stating that women are not as pure as men because of their menstruation period, so Muslim women cannot pray or fast during the holy month of Ramadhan, while their alleged emotional nature inhibits sound thinking, so they lack reason. Imam Shafi'i agrees with Hanafi on the invalidity of women's testimony in the court of law, saying: "The testimony of women is not accepted with men except in property and related matters, and the reason for this is the weakness of their intellect, and the deficiency of their accuracy, and their incapacity in ruling" (as cited in Tucker 2008, p. 141). For other Muslim scholars, women are equal to men in spiritual matters but not in economic or social issues (Roded 2008, p.3). Yet, this claim is highly contested on the Facebook pages examined in this study. One female commentator, for example, mentioned that "my family never raised me to be a weak human being who lacks reason and faith and this is what I thank Allah for. On the other hand, I met many women who were innately convinced that their status is less than that of a man which is caused by the environment, family, school, and friend. Unfortunately, these are the reasons that lead to the [degraded] current status of women." In addition, a study conducted by Gallup's World Poll in Muslim countries, the largest study of its kind, revealed that the majority of Muslim women interviewed regard Islam "as a crucial component of [their] progress," as Islam in itself is not an obstacle in pursuits of their political freedom (Esposito & Mogahed 2007, p. 114).

Another recurrent and important topic frequently discussed is the "*awra*" (taboo), as explained in Chapter 1. Facebook commentators generally refuse to regard women as "*awra*" and consider the term highly offensive. However, in Islamic jurisdiction, men should refrain from looking at women unless compelled to do so. In the case of judges and witnesses, they "should only gaze upon a woman's face with pure intentions, however, and only to fulfill their judicial responsibilities, not to fulfill their desires" (Tucker 2008, p. 182). Other posts clearly advocate women's freedom and rights, evident in recurring phrases such as "women's rights" and "the free woman," while rejecting such practices as polygamy and sexual harassment (Al-Rawi, 2014). Islam allows men to have four wives, but this topic has generated many discussions, as some posts challenged the suitability of this religious law in modern times. Again, there is a clear confrontation between secular and Islamist voices on these Facebook pages, and this online interaction can lead to cultural change.

In sum, several similar political issues are discussed in social media outlets that revolve around supporting women's freedom and rights. This is the main feature of this online form of activism. Posters generally agree that establishing secular societies wherein religion and civil laws are separated is the right decision. Though there are some anti-Islamic voices, especially in the English posts and comments, a clear distinction remains between old customs and traditions and Islamic teachings, as posters clearly differentiate between the two. Most posts blame religious men who misuse religion by issuing *fatwas* to achieve personal goals and continue to degrade women in Arab societies. Sexual harassment and the claim that women lack reason and faith are two major issues that garner great attention and discussion, as posters generally reject these notions. Finally, wearing the veil or niqab is another issue framed differently among posters. On the one hand, some posters and commentators are clearly against it, supporting their stance by suggesting that Islam never ordered women to wear it. On the other hand, another group of commentators, including females, asserted that wearing the veil is a religious obligation that should not be challenged by secularists.

In my analysis of social media posts and comments, it is important to note that several topics that recur in feminist movements in the West, such as abortion, contraception, and sexual control, do not appear to be as prominent in online discussion in the Arab world, where issues including Islam and society's perception of women and their basic freedom and equality with men are most prominent. Clearly, these are urgent matters that must be addressed. In general, three main online communities appear to be competing, either to monopolize online discussion or to gain more supporters. The first community includes the organizers of the feminist online movements and a large group of avid supporters who call for women's political freedom and rights and the importance of establishing equality among men and women in a secular society. This community has a general mistrust of religious men and old cultural beliefs sometimes justified by referring to Islam. Based on Hall's communication model, this online group occupies the hegemonic position, as the social media posts and the pages/accounts as a whole are run by them (Hall, 2001). The supporters and followers of the social movement organizers who express positive views toward this hegemonic position are included in this online community. The main point stressed by the majority of such posters and commentators is that Islam should not be blamed for the patriarchal nature of Arab societies. This stance is supported by the Gallup survey cited above, as part of the study's investigation was whether Muslim women believe Islam is linked to gender inequality. Data collected from the survey "show that there is no connection as these are mostly cultural practices that have no link to religion." More pressing issues are the focus of women's concerns, such as high unemployment and "lack of unity," while only 1% of women in Egypt, 2% in Morocco, and 5% in Saudi Arabia highlighted gender inequality (Esposito & Mogahed, 2007, pp. 122–123). In the Quran, only about six verses in a total of 6,660 discuss man's control over women (Ali, 2000, p. 43). With regard to the issue of inequality, Queen Rania of Jordan once clarified in an interview that "Islam should not be used as a scapegoat. The obstacles that face women today are more cultural. It's not about the religion" (Macleod, 2007).

A second online community, typically antagonistic toward the first community, attempts to secularize Arab societies, sometimes interpreting online movements as obscene or immoral because they deviate from the main teachings of Islam. Based on Hall's model, this online community can be categorized as the "oppositional code" because of the counter-frames or negative views expressed against the hegemonic position (Hall, 2001). I fact, some members of this online group are females who believe that wearing the veil or even the niqab is a personal choice through which women can assert their freedom and rights. In his discussion of Islamists movements, Bayat says that some devout Muslims feel that there is an ongoing attack against their religion in what he termed as a "universalising secular modernity." Also, the organizers of the "Uprising of Women in the Arab World" once revealed: "When we put up a picture of a veiled woman, no one objects to her appearance. But when we post the picture of a woman who doesn't cover herself, it is immediately plastered with comments claiming that her appearance is weakening the cause!" (RNW, 2012).

Finally, a third online community, posting mostly in English, claims that Islam is behind gender inequality in the Arab world, and members of this community generally support the social movements' organizers. As evidence of their position, they refer to the application of sharia law in Saudi Arabia in connection to women's treatment, along with selecting verses from the Quran and other Islamic teachings to support their claims. In brief, all three online communities meet in the online public sphere to exchange ideas and debate the issues cited above, though they form separate public sphericules within their three recognized clusters. Based on their ideological backgrounds, each online community frames the issue of women's rights, freedom, and equality in a way that suits its own agenda.

In conclusion, misconceptions abound on all sides, as those who advocate the cause of women's political freedom are misunderstood as promoters of obscenity and immorality even among some Muslim women, while many activists, especially in the West, believe that Islam, rather than specific cultural practices and beliefs, is behind the continued mistreatment of women. If one looks at the positive aspect of these feminist movements, it becomes clear that opportunity structures or the circumstances that occurred during and after the Arab Spring events facilitated their establishment, as through social networking sites women and men alike became further empowered to freely discuss political issues and cultural taboos in their societies without fear of being silenced or harassed. Though the actual political impact of these social movements is difficult to measure empirically, some of them clearly appear to create actual social change, or at least greater awareness, such as in the case of Oct26driving.

Chapter 5

Social Activism and Civil Society

As we have seen thus far, the proliferation of new media technologies has played an important role in empowering women involved in various types of activism. In this chapter we turn our discussion to a number of women's nongovernmental organizations (NGOs) and organizations focused on improving Arab women's social lives. The NGOs use social media to form online communities whose purpose is to raise awareness about their activities and create change through collective action. In the following paragraphs, a discussion is provided on NGOs' social media use and the benefits of creating online communities by these organizations.

Research shows that NGOs' use of social media can be very beneficial in multiple ways, such as raising awareness about social activism, building online communities with likeminded individuals from diverse geographical regions, connecting people together, and promoting collective moral and financial support (Auger, 2013; Lovejoy & Saxton, 2012; Merry, 2013; Nah, 2009, 2013; Rodriguez, 2016; Saxton, Guo, Chiu & Feng, 2012; Zhou & Pan, 2016). Rheingold, among others, believes that new technologies also assist NGOs in their humanitarian objectives:

> Nonprofits and NGOs that use CMC effectively are concrete evidence of ways this technology can be used for humanitarian purposes. Nonprofits and NGOs are organizationally well-suited to benefit from the leverage offered by CMC technology and the people power inherent in virtual communities. These groups feed people, find them medical care,

> cure blindness, free political prisoners, organize disaster relief, find shelter for the homeless—tasks as deep into human nonvirtual reality as you can get. (Rheingold, 1994)

Thousands of women's NGOs are scattered around the Arab world. For example, over 50 are active in Tunisia alone (Arab.org, n.d.). In Iraq, about 80 women's organizations and 400 NGOs deal with women's issues, though their influence is questionable, as many do not appear to be focused on tackling actual needs (ILDP, 2006, p. 38).[1] In Egypt, dozens of women's organizations attempt to coordinate activities to combat injustice and defend human rights, though some efforts have been politicized to serve the government's agenda, such as the case of the National Council of Women, which was headed by the former Egyptian president's wife before the Arab Spring events (Nazra for Feminist Studies, 2011). Some active organizations include the Egyptian Center for Women's Rights (ECWR), the New Woman Foundation, and the Women and Memory Forum (Karaoğlan, 2007, pp. 128–129). In addition, many initiatives are supported by international humanitarian organizations, such as the "Khadija" network project launched by UN Women, the European Union, and the Arab League, presumably to influence national policymakers in various countries. The goal is to "provide better work environments for women, protect them from vulnerable employment and increase women's representation in leadership positions" (UN Women, 2015–2016, p. 14). However, it is very difficult to accurately assess the effectiveness of this initiative because of the lack of data. Another point that requires attention here is the obvious antagonism between secular and Muslim NGOs, as discord is evident even on issues they both support, partly due to the influence of sectarianism and extremist groups (ILDP, 2006, p. 38).

The study of communities has been ongoing for many decades, as sociologists continue to engage with the community question (i.e., what characteristics must be present for a group to be considered a community?) (Wellman, 1979). The first studies focused on community ties with friends, relatives, and neighbors, commonly regarded as the primary sources of community support (Campbell & Lee, 1992; Wellman & Wortley, 1990). These ties are often gendered, as women commonly create connections and friendships amongst themselves based on status, such as being married, divorced, single, widowed, or elderly (O'Connor, 1992). In general, these networks create what is known as social capital—defined as "sociability, social networks and social support, trust, reciprocity, and community and civic engagement" (Morrow, 1999, p. 744)—which can be useful in providing emotional and psychological support as well as general guidance (Furstenberg & Hughes, 1995).

In terms of online communities, an early definition was provided by Howard Rheingold, who describes these communities as "cultural aggregations that emerge when enough people bump into each other often enough in cyberspace" (Rheingold, 1994, p. 57). Online communities are comprised mostly of people from diverse geographical locations (Kollock, 1999), as online presence frees users from offline obligations such as face-to-face meetings (Haythornthwaite, 2007). In general, internet users gathering in an online community aim at building a community by enhancing relationships, engagement, attachments, and discussions amongst themselves (Kavanaugh et al., 2005; Warren, Sulaiman, & Jaafar, 2014). Community members create a virtual space regarded as a safe zone for online deliberation and identity validation. This zone can be considered a subaltern public sphere (Zhang, 2012), as it provides a way to resist and counter the domination of mainstream ideas and information flows. As part of web 2.0, online communities are generally characterized as cultural platforms and distinguished by their "decentralization, shared conversation, and shared information" features (Song, 2010, p. 252). Further, members of online communities often believe that their existing social networks are enhanced by internet use, and they get to exchange ideas with those who hold opposing views (Norris, 2004). In this regard, Nessim Watson (1997) conducted an early study on Phish.Net fan community and found that its members are closely connected to each other because they are not bound by geographical distances, and there are no time constraints to hinder ongoing communication (see also Baym, 2000) Further, Wu (2014) studied Chinese online communities formed around the reality TV show Super Girl and found that they often encourage civic engagement. Indeed, the sociability and usability features of online communities are important to users (Preece & Maloney-Krichmar, 2003), while belonging to an online community and sharing ideas are attractive pursuits (Preece, 2000).

The above discussion is particularly relevant to the way online communities are organized for certain causes related to social activism (Caren, Jowers, & Gaby, 2012; Gordon, 2017), as activists can "interact, share, and converse with online members or potential members in a way that ultimately facilitates the creation of an online community with its followers" (Warren, Sulaiman, & Jaafar, 2014). For example, J. Lim studied young Malaysian activists' use of online sites like YouTube, EngageMedia, and MySpace and found that they form alternative media platforms to raise awareness about many important issues surrounding homosexuality and ethnic discrimination. As for women's causes, E. Lee (2013) conducted a study on an online diasporic community made up of female Korean immigrants in the United States. The author found that the online community can sometimes be empowering for women, such as in making them feel more independent. In what follows, a discussion is provided on four major women's NGOs, while also making reference to a few minor ones.

Women's NGOs in the Arab World

As mentioned, there are hundreds of women's NGOs and civil society organizations in the Arab world, but here we will narrow our discussion to four, chosen because they have received over 100,000 likes on Facebook. The selection was made based on several internet and Facebook searches, as well as the results of social networking analyses of women's Facebook pages. NGOs other than the four discussed are briefly referenced at the end of the chapter. The primary goal of creating social media outlets by women's NGO are related to forming online communities of likeminded people, whether men or women, who are interested in women's issues. The majority of these NGOs are able to better address their publics and garner more attention to their various causes with the assistance of new media technologies.

The first NGO we will look at is Nasawyia (النسوية) (nasawyia.org), which appears to be one of the most established NGOs that focus on women's causes in the Arab world. Its Facebook page is among the most popular (see Table 5.1). Nasawyia's headquarters is located in Haarlem in the Netherlands, and its website, which is in Arabic and English, publishes articles on contraception, women's mental health, sexually transmitted diseases, homosexuality, and general sexuality issues that are often regarded as taboo in the Arab world, as noted in Chapter 1. Incidentally, many of these topics are similar to those disseminated by the state-run Radio Netherlands Worldwide in Arabic. According to Nasawyia's website, the NGO is

Table 5.1. Social Networking Sites Cited in the Chapter

NGO	Likes/views	Link
Nasawyia	338K	www.facebook.com/Nasawyia
ABAAD	101K	www.facebook.com/abaadmena
Arab Women Campaign	2.3m	www.facebook.com/ArabWomenOfficial
Iraqi Women's Rights	130K	www.facebook.com/iraqiwomenrights

Data collected July 13, 2017.

> a feminist organization devoted to achieving full equality for women in the Middle East and North Africa through education and litigation. The organization focuses on a broad range of women's rights issues, including gender and racial discrimination, economic justice and pay equity, child marriage and female genital mutilation, honor killing, domestic violence and family law, marriage and family formation rights of same-sex couples, women's health and body image, reproductive rights, women with disabilities, representation of women in the media, and global feminist issues.

Nasawyia is run by Dareen Hasan, a Syrian female activist who made a film on Syrian refugees living in Lebanon entitled *Bread and Iron*. The organization's main goal is to empower Arab women "to break the boundaries and obtain their rights, through articles, researches, and videos that we post on social media." Interestingly, it shifted its attention from raising online awareness to multiple types of offline activities by first officially registering the organization and then working on the ground to address real needs. Their activities are numerous, but they include partnering with other local NGOs based in the MENA region to "help women undergoing domestic violence and abusive relationship there, or women fleeing honor killing and child marriages." On its YouTube channel, Hasan regularly uploads her video debates and virtual lectures with other Nasawyia's followers. The viewers can only see and hear Hasan talking, mostly in reference to women's sexual freedom, sexism, misogyny, sexual literacy, and gender stereotyping. One of the YouTube productions, "Her Fingerprint," highlights the achievements and ideas of feminist activists, including Nawal El Saadawi (see Chapter 2) and Malala Yousafzai.

To better understand the nature of the organization's activities, the researcher interviewed Dareen Hasan, who replied on June 24, 2017. She emphasizes that the organization's main concerns vary from country to country but include several important areas, such as passing laws that prohibit domestic violence and underage marriage as well as finding ways to stop online sexual harassment in many Arab countries, especially Yemen, Palestine, Egypt, and Syria. Hasan stresses that Arab countries should be examined separately because each has individual needs and differences. For example, she states that Egyptian women suffer mostly from street harassment and less from domestic violence, while many cases of incestuous rape have been cited in Palestine and Yemen. In Lebanon, the important issue is underage marriage rather than street harassment, while Syrian women suffer from all of these problems because the country is currently in a state of war, during which women are often the victims of violence. "Depending on the political and religious systems, there'll be violations against women whenever some men find venues for abuse," she claims.

Note of course that Hasan's assessment is purely personal, as no official figures exist to prove her claims. As mentioned in Chapter 1, in some of these conservative countries it is extremely difficult to collect data on sensitive topics. Plus, Hasan's assessment is based on individuals who contact her online, and large segments of society either do not have access to the internet or have not heard of Nasawyia's activities. Also, most sexual assault and rape cases end up not being reported to police, a phenomenon that exists worldwide. In short, then, while Hasan's personal assessment is important and relevant—and we have no reason to doubt its accuracy—it cannot be generalized or taken for granted.

Hasan stresses that the most common issues and frequent problems that occur in the Arab world are cyber bullying and blackmail, online sexual harassment, girls being beaten by their mothers or fathers, and incestuous rape, especially by paternal uncles and fathers. For the latter problem, girls are mostly blackmailed after rape incidents to silence them. Hasan also emphasizes that online sexual harassment often leads to suicide, such as in several cases recorded in Iraq and elsewhere. Regarding the focus of this book, Hasan confirms that mainstream media have been run and owned by men, especially those who hold masculine views, and laws have only served men by promoting what they want from women, who have been largely marginalized and treated as sexual objects. Within this context, she stresses the role social media plays in her organization, saying:

> When Facebook was introduced, it gave us a platform [for expression] and I launched Nasawyia to write whatever I like. I was able to make videos, appear on TV and radio talk shows, livestream myself, and make audio-visual materials. It's an important platform which functions like a satellite channel. Indeed, social media are so important. . . . Imagine, without Facebook no one would have known me, and my activities on the ground won't be recognized. It is also very

> important for collective action, mobilization, information dissemination, and reaching out to women who cannot watch TV or leave their houses for work or other businesses. Since such women are surrounded by men who prohibit them from moving around, they have been able to secretly use their mobile phones to get online access to these banned pages. . . . For us, it is very important to connect with those women and understand their stories which are not known in the society. Those women are also benefiting by getting psychological support, empowerment, organizing their thoughts, raising awareness, and gaining information on sexual, health and psychological issues. Social media sites have become by far the most important media platforms [in our time] because of their high engagement, free access, interactive and direct features without censorship, monitoring, deletion, or distortion.

Among the other types of affordances provided by social media is the ability to exchange mobile phone numbers to guarantee more privacy in communication. Hasan mentions, for example, that WhatsApp allows her to receive two or three daily phone calls from women who are in dire need of assistance, and the calls are treated with confidentiality to protect the identity of those women. Finally, one of the challenges faced by Nasawyia is what Hasan calls the "destructive efforts against and distortion of feminism by some women claiming to be feminists" who often attack the organization for what it stands for by forming groups to "insult and write trivial remarks" about her organization.

Nasawyia's activities are not limited to one or two MENA countries, as they are scattered all over the region; its topics are of interest to diverse audiences. Also, the online community the NGO created is typically not bound by geographical borders. In fact, an examination of the NGO's Facebook followers indicate they are located in different Arab states, with Egypt ranking first, followed by Syria, Morocco, and Iraq (SocialBakers, 2017). This geographical diversity is confirmed by Hasan, who adds that the majority of her followers are between 13 and 35 years old, and that women constitute about 64% of users.

Examining Nasawyia's Facebook page, we find that the most-liked posts are mainly positive in nature and aimed at empowering women. Other top Facebook posts include references to the campaign for supporting the LGBTQ community in Syria with the hashtag (#You're not alone) and (#MTVSyriaLoveWins), as well as mixed-gender prayers at a mosque in San Francisco. Interestingly, the NGO uses Facebook to interact with audiences as well as taking their opinions on different matters. Nasawyia borrows posts from the "Uprising of Women in the Arab World" (whose campaign is discussed in Chapter 4), exhibiting the complementary efforts some NGOs are exerting to raise awareness about women's issues and human right. The Facebook page also lists "masculine crimes" or news about discrimination and hate crimes against women in the Arab world. Other popular Facebook posts deal with news stories on violent domestic abuse, gang rapes, and honor killings, often containing graphic images and details. Most of these posts emphasize the injustice women face in the legal system and the mistreatment they receive in society due to its patriarchal nature.[2] In brief, the objective of using social media outlets by Nasawyia is to create an online community whose core values are centered on activism and social change. Safe spaces are also provided for members to interact with each other and with the head of the NGO to become more aware of women's issues and seek solutions to their urgent problems and concerns.

The second NGO we will look at here is ABAAD (Dimensions) (أبعاد). This organization, based in Lebanon (www.abaadmena.org), is supported by several NGOs and international humanitarian organizations; it describes itself as follows:

> A non-profit, non-politically affiliated, non-religious civil association founded in June 2011 with the aim of promoting sustainable social and economic development in the MENA region through equality, protection, and empowerment of marginalised groups, especially women. ABAAD comprises of a dynamic pool of resources, human rights activists, lawyers, experts in their fields, social workers, and researchers that are all dedicated towards achieving gender equality and women's empowerment.

The NGO has an emergency number for women and children seeking immediate intervention and assistance from domestic abuse who can benefit from its safe house called Al Dar (House). The main focus of ABAAD is Lebanon, and particularly the issue of the Lebanese underage marriage law, for which the organization has mobilized social media followers and lobbied officials, with the goal of getting certain laws changed.

Followers on ABAAD's Facebook page are mostly from Lebanon, Egypt, and Tunisia. This sequence of geographical locations is also confirmed by the email interview cited below with ABAAD's director of programs. In terms of most-liked posts, data retrieved from the Facebook page indicates the top post is a women's empowerment video entitled "Ending violence is possible," which deals with the personal accounts of three Arab women: Zeina, Hala, and Sarah, who have survived domestic violence and abuse from their husbands. A passage that accompanies the video states:

> Today women are not just numbers. Today women are unique individuals, and not labeled as "victims" of violence.
>
> Today, Zeina Hala and Sarah bravely share with us their ordeal. They courageously share with us their ability to overcome violence.
>
> Today, we are all Zeina, Hala and Sarah!
>
> Meet them and listen to their stories, with no masks.

The second most-liked post, which is also the most commented-on one, relates to another video regarding proposed Bill 522 in Lebanon that stipulates the following: "Any rapist will not be persecuted if he marries his female victim." The description of the video states, in Arabic and English: "This is not a promotional video, but it is the reality of a woman's feeling towards marrying her rapist [in Arabic]. Who does the Lebanese law protect? The victim or the rapist? Abolish Bill 522 now! [in English]." The statement is followed by two hashtags that the Facebook page's followers are encouraged to circulate, including #Undress522 and #abolish522. Several similar statements are found in the data analyzed, as the third most-liked post is an online petition accompanied by a GIF image with the statement: "Every signature tells the Parliament that White [dress] will never cover the rape! [*sic*] Sign the petition now and let your voice be heard loud and clear. Undress522.com." Finally, the second most commented-on post, an image used as the Facebook page profile, states that "Every 'yes' from you is regarded as 'no' for every rapist. Vote to revoke 522 Bill #Don't make us adopt 522." It is obvious here that the NGO is trying to collectively mobilize its social media followers, especially those living in Lebanon, to pressure the government to stop processing Bill 522.

In a June 15 and 16, 2017, interview, Roula El Masri, the Gender Equality Program Director at ABAAD, provided further details about the NGO. The majority of its Facebook page followers are between 18 and 34 years old, and 59% of them are women. Due to the influence of globalization, the preferred language used is English, followed by Arabic and French. In terms of online moderation, "ABAAD allows people to post their views even if they contradict the NGO's mandate," yet "posts that are obscene or insulting are deleted," according to El Masri. As for the role of media in connection to the most urgent issues that the NGO aims at addressing, El Masri says that it tries to "mobilize the public on a national level in order to shape the foundation of public opinion and stop violence against women and girls." The organization also attempts to "build women's capacity and develop their leadership and negotiation skills which can be useful if they become policy makers." Finally, ABAAD uses various platforms and tools to "support women refugees in making short films about their living conditions, while social media are utilized to promote these efforts."

In brief, social media outlets provide the NGO with many affordances, including "disseminating special messages about violence and women's rights to a large array of national, regional, and international audiences." Second, they provide plenty of women with "a platform to raise their voice and freely express their opinions about issues they suffer from like violence and discrimination." Also, they help in "establishing and enhancing means of communication among different women and individuals to exchange experiences and skills." Finally, social media outlets assist in "shaping public opinion and exerting pressure as well as mobilizing [people] to support social campaigns on political and legal reforms."

As for addressing the most urgent needs in MENA countries, El Masri mentions that "the patriarchal and masculine culture which is the norm" explains the kind of stark discrimination against women that exists in many MENA countries. Yet there are "some differences such as the case of Syria, Palestine, Iraq, and Yemen wherein women face double the amount of discrimination as well as domestic and sexual abuse" because of their unique circumstances due to civil war and armed conflict. Other Arab countries such as Saudi Arabia, Mauritania, and

Sudan do not have clear definitions of sexual violence and domestic abuse, while women also face discrimination in citizenship laws, as their children or husbands cannot become naturalized citizens except in Morocco, Tunisia, and Algeria. Note that, similar to Dareen Hasan's account above, El Masri's assessment is also limited in scope because it is based on a general understanding of women's needs in the MENA region, but the two agree that prominent problems exist in certain Arab countries due to their unique sociopolitical and economic circumstances. Finally, El Masri lists the most significant challenges faced by ABAAD:

1. The established patriarchal structure that exists in local cultures.
2. The lack of political stability and security that affect the sustainability of continuing activities.
3. The way some women in local cultures normalize domestic abuse.
4. Giving priority to financial and economic needs and regarding the issue of violence against women as marginal, especially in the context of refugee crisis and wars.
5. The reliance of civil society organizations on financial aid (instead of finding other resources) to sustain their programs and activities.
6. The [problematic] stance of some women's organizations as related to gender equality and the issue of discrimination against women.

Regarding points 3 and 6, El Masri clearly blames some women and their organizations as partly behind the challenges faced in creating gender equality in the MENA region. Incidentally, this is a similar claim to one Hasan makes, as both partly blame some women to be behind their own plight.

The third NGO we will discuss is the "Arab Women Campaign," which aids in running a TV show called "The Queen TV" (thequeen.tv), launched in 2015. This is the first pageant competition for the "Queen of Social Responsibilities," which has its own YouTube channel. The concept of the competition was conceived by Mustapha Salamah and Rihab Zain Aldeen in Cairo during the 2014 Mundial for Media and Artistic Productions. The goal is to enhance the collective sense of social responsibilities around the Arab world by inviting 40 or so young Arab women (between 20 and 40 years) to participate and market their civil society projects. The TV show airs on more than 30 Arab TV and 16 FM radio channels around the MENA region.

The Arab Women Campaign's motto since 2006 has been "Media for the sake of serving women." The NGO is supervised by the Arab Union for TV Productions, which is part of the Arab League and allegedly intends to use media to address women's causes around the Arab world. According to its website, the Arab Women Campaign has no political, sectarian, or religious goals, though it is very hard to trust this statement because of the media censorship and advocacy that exists in most parts of the Arab world. The campaign is credited with launching the program "The Ideal Woman," which aired on 70 channels, awarding prizes to 240 distinguished women from various Arab countries. Other TV programs launched by the NGO include "White Hands Drama," which covered the concerns of Arab women and the challenges they face; the "Talent Team," which tours several universities to make use of skilled students in producing programs that serve the causes of Arab women; "Women News Agency," an online platform dealing with news on Arab women (www.wonews.net); "The Woman Model Medal," an annual prize awarded to a distinguished figure who has made a positive change in women's lives; and "The Arab Woman's Parliament," a 2017 initiative concerned with social responsibility issues around the Arab world.

This NGO's Facebook page reveals minimal audience engagement. It appears the Facebook page organizers allow anyone to post, which explains the many irrelevant articles and images that include unrelated print commercials. Despite the apparently good intentions of the Arab Women Campaign, it airs its TV programs and shows on mainstream media, making it impossible to tackle urgent issues and taboos such as sexual harassment, underage marriage, female genital mutilation, slavery, and prostitution because these media outlets are censored and controlled by Arab governments and/or bodies that do not allow controversial issues to be covered (Amin, 2002; Fandy, 2007; Khazen, 1999; Martin, Martins, & Wood, 2016). Further, there is a clear economic incentive in airing the TV shows; for example, audience voting for the best contestant for the "Queen of Social Responsibilities" can be done only through sites that cost money instead of outlets that are free of charge. In brief, the Queen TV program is very popular on Facebook, but it seems to pay lip service to serving women's causes, as it remains a show business that is limited in scope due to its reliance on mainstream media and official sponsors. The campaign serves the economic interests of certain groups and TV channels rather than addressing actual women's concerns and problems. Instead of relying on grassroots organizations, the Arab Women Campaign is tied to political powers; for instance, the prize for "The Woman Model Medal" was awarded to a member of the Emirati Royal family rather than an Arab activist working on the ground.

Finally, the fourth NGO we will look at is "Iraqi Women's Rights" (IWR), based in Copenhagen, Denmark. IWR does not have an official website, instead relying almost entirely on social media. The goal of this NGO is to raise awareness about all types of injustice practiced against women in Iraq, its main target group (though some Facebook users follow the NGO from other Arab countries, including Egypt and Jordan), as confirmed by the interview cited below. Note that the Iraqi women diaspora living in neighboring countries might explain the followers from other countries despite the limited national focus of this NGO.

Among its main activities, IWR strives to stop violence and discrimination against Iraqi women and to defend their right to equal education and freedom of opinion and expression. According to its Facebook page, the NGO's mission is "essential and basic which is preventing the marginalization of Iraqi women by a patriarchal and rigid society. We want women to have a say in determining their future, which means they have the absolute authority to choose their lives' paths." In interviews with Thuraya Rufaat, the CEO of Iraqi Women's Rights, on May 27 and June 10, 2017, she mentioned that most of the problems that women discuss with the NGO are "related to domestic abuse." Rufaat is a woman activist and works as a telecommunication engineer, claiming that the NGO is not supported by any side or official body because it is self-funded. She thinks that violence is a widespread phenomenon, as it is "the only shared element in all the calls we receive which includes physical, psychological, and sexual assaults. Street harassment also constitutes a large number of these problems." Together with other activists, they are trying to expand the organization to be able to address more urgent issues on the ground since as of now the organization exists only on social media. For example, Rufaat says that IWR wants to "provide safe houses because there are none available in Iraq which can offer women and their children protection [from domestic violence]. In addition, the NGO wants to lobby the government to pass laws against sexual harassment and underage marriage." On IWR's Facebook page, Rufaat states:

> It has served the NGO a great deal especially that it is based outside Iraq. Social networking sites helped in conveying the views and ideas of IWR. They also assist many women to connect with us and communicate their suffering as many of them are subjected to great amounts of violence; some of whom cannot leave their homes and use traditional telecommunication means [e.g., phone calls] to report their sufferings.

Rufaat also refers to the kind of interactions on Facebook, stating that some men attack the NGO's mission and ideas, accusing it of "corrupting the girls' minds and agitating them to rebel," though some women also attack the NGO for the same reasons. Rufaat considers these women "victims of the patriarchal nature of the society because they are resisting those who want to free them from masculine chains." This is very similar to the point cited above by El Masri from ABAAD and Dareen Hasan from Nasawyia. The most important challenges the NGO faces include changing the ideas of the mainstream culture; for example, the concept of freedom is "defined as loose behavior, immorality, and nakedness, and the NGO is frequently accused of that though we call for freedom of thought, living, and practicing daily life like choosing your life partner or [even] your field of study."

Analysis of IWR's Facebook page reveals that its posts are focused on highlighting the injustices and challenges faced by Iraqi women, including stereotyping and prejudice against women. For example, there are several posts and images of Afrah Shawki, an Iraqi journalist who campaigned against government corruption; in late 2016 she was kidnapped by an unknown armed group allegedly connected to Iraqi security forces and held for 9 days before her release (AFP, 2016; BBC News, 2016b). Regarding most-liked posts, they deal with praising the professional achievements of a number of Arab women who also take care of their families and children, such as Tamara Shakir and Raya Abi

Rashid, both well-known media figures. The post, however, communicates a rather ironic tone, stating: "Behind every successful woman, a man who tried to destroy her in the name of love but failed." Another top post is related to a woman's reaction to the hashtag "a man assaults his wife in the south" (see Chapter 6), which defended the action of an Iraqi man who abused his wife in front of his daughter. The post, intended to shame the woman who defended the action of the abusive man, states: "There is nothing worse that a woman who takes a stance against her own gender with all this ignorance and degradation."

As for IWR's Facebook page social networking map, the NGO is connected to some popular regional and local pages, such as Ghada Al Saman, Ahlam Mosteghanemi, Egyptian Women Union, "Black suits you," The Uprising of Women in the Arab World, Iraqi Women, and "No to All Forms of Violence against Women and Girls," as well as international organizations, associations, and bodies like UNICEF, Women's Rights News, and Say No—UNiTE to end violence against women. Relying on Gephi software, analysis clearly shows that many women's NGOs are closely connected, indicating common interest in exchanging views and news as well as in supporting common initiatives.

Indeed, as mentioned at the beginning of the chapter, there are hundreds of social media initiatives on women's issues launched by local NGOs and online communities in the Arab world, including the Feminist Arab Men, "Woman is a Revolution not Shame" (المرأة ثورة و ليست عورة), and "Iraqi Liberal Women" (متحررات عراقيات) online community, where the motto is "Yes for freedom to women." Regarding the latter, the Facebook page organizer, who often cites well-known liberal thinkers such as Nawal El Saadawi, Ali Al-Wardi, and Nazar Qabani, frequently attacks sexual harassments, underage marriage, religious hypocrisy, domestic violence, and women wearing niqab. There are many references to the Uprising of Women in the Arab World, while screenshots from fiery messages sent by men who oppose the idea of the "Iraqi Liberal Women" community are often posted on the Facebook page to shame them as well as discredit their claims. For example, one screenshot lists the following comments from users: (1) "Why don't you say that the secret behind the society's degradation is women. Your evil schemes are profound" (2) "Adam followed God's orders. If Eve hasn't eaten it, all human beings would have been in Heaven." (3) "Allah curses you and your family. You're debased and arrogant. [I] spit on you" (4) "Iraqi Liberal Women," can you send me your porn video? I hope we can practice shadda [gang rape you]. We're waiting." These offensive messages provide insight into the way some people, primarily men from the MENA region, misunderstand the concepts of "liberal thought" and "freedom of ideas" in connection to women. This is similar to Thuraya Rufaat's comments above about the numerous accusations her NGO receives.

More recently, human rights activists and online grassroots efforts like the ones cited above have actually succeeded in raising awareness about the rape culture in the Arab world. Some of these efforts have led to abolishing a law in 2017 that allowed rapists to marry their victims if they wanted to escape punishment in Egypt, Morocco, and Tunisia (Osman, 2017; Roberts, 2017). Other Arab countries, such as Lebanon and Jordan, followed their lead and abolished the same law (BBC News, 2017a). Online users praised the Jordanian government through the use of the #308Removed hashtag for changing Article 308, which stipulated a provision similar to that of Bill 522 in Lebanon (BBC News, 2017b). However, a total of 159 convicted rapists managed to avoid imprisonment in Jordan from 2010 and 2013 as a result of this controversial law (The New Arab, 2017).

In conclusion, the NGOs discussed here all have limitations, be they in the scope of their activism or their geographical focus. For example, the most popular NGO on social media, the Arab Women Campaign, does not truly address real women's problems, as its main focus is providing a promotional platform for powerful political figures such as the Emirati royal family (the AWC is based in Dubai). Nasawyia, on the other hand, is more inclusive than the others, which probably explains its popularity; however, it is located outside the Arab world, and its direct impact might be less effective than that of ABAAD, which is based in Lebanon. It is true that globalization and the use of social media outlets facilitated a great deal of communication and connection among people, but there remain real local needs on the ground that must be addressed. Nasawyia, Iraqi Women's Rights, and the Center for Women's Equality are all based in Europe, so their actual impact can be more linked to changing misconceptions on women's status and raising awareness on human rights in the long run rather than addressing their immediate and short-term needs.

It remains difficult to quantitatively assess the true impact of these NGOs, but they are certainly raising national and regional awareness concerning many significant women's issues and causes.

More importantly, the social media platforms and mobile outlets of different women NGOs provide safe spaces to form tightly knit online communities that allow them to get vital advice and assistance that can sometimes save the lives of victims of domestic or sexual violence. That said, the interviews discussed in this chapter indicate that a perhaps surprising number of women in the Arab world are actively trying to undermine the efforts of achieving equal rights with men, mostly due to religious beliefs and the influence of patriarchal and masculine values on their lives.

Chapter 6

Cultural Activism and Anti-Violence Campaigns

In this chapter our focus moves to several social media awareness campaigns that have appeared in the Arab world dealing with women's cultural activism, especially related to sexual violence and harassment. I argue here that the general goal of these campaigns is to change some of the old cultural practices associated with women's lived experiences with the use of cultural productions. Cultural activism is defined in different ways, with no general agreement on its meaning (Grindon, 2011, p. 21), but it refers primarily to the way cultural productions such as billboards, posters, and videos are used to raise awareness about pressing societal and political issues to create positive change (Li, 2007; Smith, 1997). There is no doubt that new media technologies as well as the internet have "ushered in a revolution in cultural activism" (Leistyana, 2008, p. 708), and this chapter provides insight into the way new media in particular is used to raise awareness, create a network for social support, and make mobilizing action possible. The campaigns we will look at include "KAFA [enough] Violence and Exploitation" and "What is hidden is worse," which deal with sexual exploitation and domestic abuse as well as tweets and YouTube videos and comments on sexual harassment.

As discussed in Chapter 1, the general situation of Arab women is not up to international standards due to the difficulties they face in almost every facet of their lives (Abadeer, 2015). About "37% of Arab women have experienced some form of violence in their lifetime," though the true figure might be much higher than this (UN Women, n.d.). As for underage marriage, about 700 million living women married under the age of 18. Fourteen percent of "Arab girls marry under the age of 18. Rapists are often shown leniency or even acquitted in the Arab Region if they married their victims" (UN Women, n.d.). Another study found that between 2013 and 2015, 52% of Yemen girls were married under the age of 15, representing 65% of all marriages, and the age of the married child does not exceed 8 or 10 years in some cases (UN Women, 2013a, p. 16). In fact, "there are 8 girl child deaths per day in Yemen because of early marriage and early pregnancy and birth in the absence of the necessary health requirements for marriage" (ibid.).[1] However, there is not enough field research in the area of sexual violence and harassment in the Arab world, mostly due to cultural taboos around sexuality matters and the fact that many Arab governments do not invest enough efforts, money, and time on these important issues.[2]

Further, around 200 million girls between the ages of 15 and 49 years have been forced to undergo female genital mutilation or circumcision. It is important to note here that female genital mutilation is a cultural practice, and neither Islam nor Christianity has any stipulations or rules regarding it. In the Arab world, female genital mutilation or circumcision is most prevalent in Somalia (98%), Djibouti (93%), Egypt (91%), Eritrea (89%), Sudan (88%), Mauritania (69%), Yemen (23%), and Kurdistan, in northern Iraq (8%) (UNICEF, 2013), though some of these percentages may be exaggerated. In a more recent report by UNICEF (2016), some minor improvements have been observed, but vast challenges remain. For example, from 2004 to 2015, girls and women between the ages of 15 and 49 years have undergone female genital mutilation in Somalia (98%), Djibouti (93%), Egypt (87%), Sudan (87%), Eritrea (83%), Mauritania (69%), Yemen (19%), and Kurdistan in northern Iraq (8%). Also, during the same time period, 2004 to 2015, girls aged 0 to 14 years have undergone female circumcision in Eritrea (33%), Sudan (32%), Yemen (15%), and Egypt (14%) (UNICEF, 2016). In a national survey conducted in Egypt, about 50% of women respondents believed that female genital mutilation needs to continue because it is a religious requirement (United Nations, 2013). As can be seen from the figures above, there are clear disparities among Arab countries in relation to this cultural practice, which provides an indication into the differences in local values and beliefs, as many other Arab countries do not practice or encourage female genital mutilation or circumcision.

Meanwhile, many international humanitarian organizations are engaged in "more pressing" matters, such as providing aid for refugees and victims of war, though there are often overlaps and lack of coordination among national civil society groups, which can make it more difficult to get an accurate overview. For example, "data on domestic violence tend to rely on records of organizations that provide services for victims. Given that each organization uses its own system for registering cases, there is no common reference system to avoid registering the same victim more than once" (United Nations, 2013, p. 33). Further, data on forced prostitution, kidnappings and disappearances, honor killings, and women's slavery is almost nonexistent, as news reports are scattered on these important issues, and there is no way to understand the full picture based on the available sources. An example, from 2014, is the Islamic State in Iraq and Syria (ISIS) enslaving thousands of Yazidi women because they were not Muslims; no available numbers can be relied on to fully gauge the magnitude of this horrific incident (Jalabi, 2014; Spencer, 2014).

Among primary sources of information are national surveys conducted in certain Arab countries on sexual harassment and violence against women. For instance, about 9,000 cases of abuse have been documented in Algeria; two-thirds of these involved the husband as the initiator of aggression, the majority of them occurring in front of children. Some of the reported cases involved sexual abuse (5%) or rape (3%). The survey found that women who have low education and unpaid employment were more likely to be subjected to verbal and physical violence.

In Egypt, about 30% of women believe that their husbands can beat them if they leave the house without permission, reject sexual intercourse requests, or neglect their children (United Nations, 2013, p. 2). This corresponds with another study conducted by UN Women and Promundo, which provided answers to certain questions on gender roles and decision making, violence, and masculinity and femininity, including whether women deserve to be beaten. Respondents from four Arab countries who agreed or strongly agreed with the permissibility of beating women were as follows: Egypt, men 53.4%, women 32.8%; Morocco, men 38.2%, women 20.6%; Palestine, men 34%, women 26%; Lebanon, men 21%, women 5%. These results closely correspond to responses from interviews reported in Chapter 5, wherein some women are partly blamed for their plight. The other relevant question asked in the survey is whether a woman should tolerate violence to keep the family together. The respondents who agreed or strongly agreed with this statement were as follows: Egypt, men 90%, women 70.9%; Morocco, men 62.2%, women 45.9%; Palestine, men 63%, women 50%; Lebanon, men 26%, women 14% (Promundo & UN Women, 2017).

In Iraq, the Society of Physicians for Human Rights conducted a survey in 2003 on domestic violence, which found that half the female and male respondents agreed that a husband has the right to beat his wife if she disobeys him (ILDP, 2006, p. 86). In another survey conducted by the same organization in southern Iraq, 50% of the sample from 2000 households stated that domestic violence is manifested in beatings, torture and even murder, and the majority of female victims do not receive the medical treatment they required (ILDP, 2006, p. 86). Another health survey conducted in Iraq between 2006 and 2007 covered the controlling behavior of husbands, which was confirmed by 83% of female respondents. Other types of violence reported included emotional (33%); physical, defined as "beating, burning, choking, threatening or attacking with a knife" (21%); and violence during pregnancy (14%) (United Nations, 2013). National surveys from other Arab countries are relevant to this chapter, but space constraints precludes listing them all here. I, the author, am originally from Iraq, and I can confirm that rape culture and street harassment there are thriving, and sometimes even praised. For instance, a word in Iraqi dialect, "shaddah" (knot), refers to a man's girlfriend being gang raped by his friends. Some men claim shaddah is a source of pride or victory, often stating that the woman deserves it because it was her mistake to go alone to her boyfriend's home. Of course, the victim almost always remains silent for fear of family punishment or social shame. The word "rape" is not even mentioned in this context, which is another way of justifying its occurrence. As for street harassment, it occurs daily in Iraq, often reaching the level of verbal insults and physical and sexual assaults against women, especially in public spaces and crowded religious sites. Despite the lack of evidence on sexual harassment and violence against women, the general indicators cited above provide important insight into the challenging conditions of women in the Arab world. As a result, many social media campaigns and online initiatives have been launched to promote cultural activism to change the situation. The following section presents a discussion on the theory of social media affordances as related to the way new media provides opportunities for people and organizations to achieve their cultural activism goals.

Social Media Affordances

As explained above, the general condition of women in the Arab world is not encouraging based on international standards, and this difficult situation affects many areas, including legal rights, education, health, and equal employment opportunities. As a reaction, many social campaigns in the Arab world have employed social media outlets to raise cultural awareness about injustice, empower women to talk freely, and attempt to find solutions to their pressing issues. Indeed, one of the benefits of using social media is its affordances, a concept explained here.

In his original theory of affordances, which is part of ecological psychology discipline, James Gibson mentions that the environment affords people many benefits to enhance communication and interaction (1986). The word itself was coined by Gibson in the pre-Internet era to refer to the complementary nature of people (users) and their environment (social media in this context), and many scholars have employed the theory to explain the way social media provides functional tools for their users to further communicate and interact (Enjolras, Steen-Johnsen, & Wollebæk, 2013; Halpern & Gibbs, 2013). In other words, a symbiotic relationship binds users and technology, as the latter's affordance is related to "the mutuality of actor intentions and technology capabilities that provide the potential for a particular action" (Faraj & Azad, 2012). Studies show that people who are part of a large network are more likely to talk and share ideas (Huckfeldt, Mendez & Osborn, 2004; McLeod et al., 1999). This is because networks provide different types of support through various channels of communication (Kim, 2014; Li, Chen, & Popiel, 2015). Social support, which is connected to the well-being of individuals, can be defined as "the perception or reception of coping assistance or as attributes of one's social circle" (Meng, Martinez, Holmstrom, Chung, & Cox, 2017, p. 1). In fact, social support is regarded as one of the most important affordances (Butler, 2001; Hall & Wellman, 1985; Wellman & Wortley), which connects to our discussion in Chapter 5 on the benefits of creating online communities. In a strong network, social support can improve mental health and well-being (Schaefer, Coyne, & Lazarus, 1981), also evident in the case of internet use and online communities (Idriss, Kvedar, & Watson, 2009; Leung, 2006; Shaw & Gant, 2002), as well as social media use (Cheung, Chiu, & Lee, 2011; Frison & Eggermont, 2015; Kim & Lee, 2011; Meng et al., 2017; Nabi, Prestin, & So, 2013).

In general, the different types of functional affordances are similar to the arguments made about the uses and gratification theory (LaRose, Mastro & Eastin, 2001). Lin (1999), for example, notes that internet use has several functions, including surveillance, escape, companionship, identity, and entertainment. Indeed, finding companionship and enhancing one's connections are relevant to the scope of this chapter. Social media affordances also provide users with tools to understand their environment and benefit from its affordances, such as seeing "who else is in a chat room, who was co-sent a message, or who are the friends of my friends on a social network site" (Hogan & Quan-Haase, 2010). It also includes making use of likeminded users in a network to further spread the word; getting identity validation, such as that related to feminist issues; and receiving psychological and moral support when needed. Social media affordances also include making use of status updates, often used to get feedback and validation from others (Hampton et al., 2011a). Feedback might come from offline sources, such as phone calls or in-person meetings, which "provide an awareness of the attentiveness of others to one's need for support" (Lu & Hampton, 2017). Zheng and Yu referred to this theory in their study of the Free Lunch for Children program in China launched on Weibo. The authors linked the theory of collective action to affordances-for-practice concept, while Halpern and Gibbs (2013) used the theory to explain how social media can be a catalyst for online deliberation. Majchrzak and colleagues (2013) examined how information sharing can be turned via use of social media into "a continuous online knowledge conversation of strangers, unexpected interpretations and re-uses, and dynamic emergence," especially in providing four types of affordances: metavoicing, triggered attending, network-informed associating, and generative role taking (2013). In brief, media campaigns dealing with women's issues in the Arab world can be considered important tools for cultural activism in the way they build strong connections among users interested in mutual topics, while social media affordances make it possible to empower women and others to speak about their cultural concerns to raise awareness and create appropriate support for themselves and their causes. In the following section, data retrieved from social media such as YouTube and campaigns dealing with sexual harassment and violence against women is presented and analyzed.

Anti-Violence and Sexual Harassment on Social Media

In this section we focus on several social media campaigns in Arab countries, using criteria such as popularity, media coverage, and cultural impact. On Twitter, I searched for tweets using the term "harassment" in Arabic (تحرش) for one month (May 29 to June 29, 2017) and collected a total of 25,443 tweets posted by 6,216 unique users. Most (16,739, or 65.7%) related to one particular post: "[Sexually] harasses a veiled girl in a public place by showing his penis and placing it on her hand." The tweet is usually accompanied by a blurred picture of a man's penis; most of the tweets are meant to depict, distribute, and highlight sexually explicit content rather than condemning the alleged act, while male users are often involved in spreading such tweets. This can be a reflection and online extension of the rape and patriarchal culture that exists in the region.

The second most-retweeted post (599 tweets) discusses an allegation of sexual harassment by a taxi driver working for Careem car company in Saudi Arabia. A Saudi woman took a video with her mobile phone of the taxi driver, who was allegedly performing "an obscene act," possibly masturbating in his taxi. Most of these retweets are meant to discredit the claim, while a few others intend to highlight the suffering of Saudi women who are forced to take taxis instead of driving themselves to work. Hundreds of other tweets exist that deal with allegations of sexual and domestic harassments in different Arab countries. Many other hashtags deal with domestic abuse, such as "#a man assaults his wife in the south," which occurred in early February 2017 in Saudi Arabia and became the trending hashtag for a while. The man started beating his wife in front of his daughter in public, and the wife posted a video of her abuse while lying on a hospital bed (Al Sadawi, 2017). The trending hashtag encouraged other women to tweet about their own experiences and create an online debate on how to defend women from abusive husbands. This shows that Twitter functions as an online public sphere for cultural activism due to the affordances it provides wherein urgent issues not usually reported in mainstream media are vigorously discussed.

In a second search, this time on YouTube, I sought occurrences of the Arabic term for sexual harassment (التحرش الجنسي). After removing duplicates, this search yielded 520 videos, with 20,848 comments. I then performed two analyses. First, I examined the top 10 most-viewed and commented-on video clips (see Table 6.1); second, I analyzed the comments using QDA Miner–Word Stat software to understand the general topics of the YouTube audience. Since this study is focused on women in the Arab world, videos on sexual assault that happened elsewhere or harassment against children have not been included in the discussion on videos. For example, the second most-viewed video is "'Sexual harassment against children' starring the actress Oraib," which is an official production of the Abu Dhabi Judicial Department. The same video with a slightly different title is also the eighth most-viewed clip in the sample; hence, these videos have not been included in my account below.

Based on video analysis, the most-viewed video has received over 18 million views, and is also the ninth most-commented on clip. Dealing with a comparison between Egypt in the 1970s and today, its producer borrowed a clip from two Egyptian movies made in 1970s and 2000s, stating: "Two scenes from two ages that sum up everything." The footage from the old movie shows how an unveiled Egyptian woman defends herself from a male sexual harasser in a public bus, after which other passengers support her and corner the harasser. The more recent footage shows a veiled woman confronting her male sexual harasser by pricking him with a needle; other male passengers support the harasser and attack the woman for harming the man, who claims she is "crazy." The main point of the YouTube video is to indicate the change in Egyptian cultural values, as sexual harassment has become normalized in recent times. The film producer asks in the end, "What happened to Egypt?" Aside from the difference in the people's reaction, the two women are distinguished from each other in that the second one is veiled, which supposedly sends the message that she observes the society's conservative rules, and yet this has not prevented harassment. Egyptian society has evolved to become more misogynistic, masculine, and intolerant toward women, mostly seen after the Arab Spring events, an intolerance that has also occurred in other countries, such as Tunisia (Coleman, 2011). Overall, this video production functions as cultural activism, with a goal of raising awareness and creating change.

The third most-viewed video, "Sexual harassment in Egypt +18 for adults only—Distribute," was posted by Ahmed Elshoboksy. The poster has a popular YouTube talk show in which he discusses incidents of sexual harassment in Egypt, some of which show police

Table 6.1. The Top 10 Most-Viewed and Most Commented-On Videos on Sexual Harassment

	Video ID	Channel Title	Title	Views
1.	6A0n4_8nGTw	mahmoud arafat	ماذا جرى لمصر؟..التحرش الجنسي. [What happened to Egypt? . . . Sexual harassment]	18,964,710
2.	ASngw779b2c	ADJD_Official	الفيلم القصير ‹التحرش الجنسي بالأطفال› من بطولة الفنانة عريب [The short film "sexual harassment against children" starring the actress, Oraib]	6,084,439
3.	isj7St9pc0c	Ahmed Elshobokshy	التحرش الجنسي في مصر 18+ للكبار فقط –انشرها [Sexual harassment in Egypt +18 for adults only—Distribute]	5,984,480
4.	noAJy7z0vXo	عيال ابوطالب	التحرش الجنسي عيني عينك [Sexual harassment without shame]	4,757,066
5.	WDg36HwH3Uc	settat onchat	فيلم سلمى عن التحرش الجنسي [Selma film on sexual harassment]	3,540,445
6.	e5hbw1pWV6E	e3lamakTV	تجربة مثيرة عن التحرش الجنسي في مصر - شاب يرتدي زي فتاة و ينزل إلي الشارع و يتم التحرش به [An interesting experiment on sexual harassment in Egypt—a man wearing women's clothes, walks in the street, and gets sexually harassed]	3,088,900
7.	LhYPW4YBBRY	bestchannel2014	عاقبة التحرش الجنسي - شاهد ماالذي حصل لشاب يتحرش بفتاة [Punishment of sexual harassment—see what happened to a boy who sexually harassed a girl]	2,769,520
8.	hvayRahNbHw	Oraib-عريب حمدان Hamdan	الفيلم التوعوي التحرش الجنسي بالأطفال - تمثيل الفنانة عريب [The educational film "sexual harassment against children" by the actress, Uraib]	2,565,770
9.	6wVnO6M9r7w	Nawaat	كلام شارع : التونسي و التحرش الجنسي [Street talk: The Tunisian and sexual harassment]	2,302,278
10.	2BUdi4_arxU	VideoYoum7 | قناة اليوم السابع	التحرش الجنسي داخل مراكب النيل [Sexual harassment inside Nile's boats]	1,956,844

continued on next page

Table 6.1. Continued.

	Video ID	Channel Title	Title	Comments
1.	ZyOmkGRtIjM	Fahad Sal	تحرش_بفتاتين_بجدة | التحرش الجنسي# [Sexual harassment: Harassing two girls in Jaddah#]	5,078
2.	e6hbw1pWV6E	e3lamakTV	تجربة مثيرة عن التحرش الجنسي في مصر - شاب يرتدي زي فتاة و ينزل إلي الشارع و يتم التحرش به [An interesting experiment on sexual harassment in Egypt—a man wearing women's clothes, walks in the street, and gets sexually harassed]	4,354
3.	ZVBV69g8TS4	Nmkosour l نَمْكُوصُور	نمكوصور | تحرش جنسي بالأطفال [Nmkosour: Sexual harassment against children]	2,286
4.	M_IY3FEG2Hg	ilyass Lakhrissi	الشيخ سار - التحرش الجنسي - برنامج Génération News الحلقة كاملة- بجودة جيدة [Sheikh Sar: Sexual harassment: Generation News show, complete episode, good quality]	1,581
5.	6wVnO6M9r7w	Nawaat	كلام شارع : التونسي و التحرش الجنسي [Street talk: The Tunisian and sexual harassment]	1,174
6.	2BUdi4_arxU	VideoYoum7 | قناة اليوم السابع	التحرش الجنسي داخل مراكب النيل [Sexual harassment inside Nile's boats]	605
7.	hvayRahNbHw	Oraib-عريب حمدان Hamdan	الفيلم التوعوي التحرش الجنسي بالأطفال - تمثيل الفنانة عريب [The educational film "sexual harassment against children" by the actress, Oraib]	552
8.	1_evQcPTxDY	جحيم الحقيقة	التحرش الجنسي بلاطفال البزرنجية +18 [Sexual harassment against children of Bazranjiah +18]	460
9.	6A0n4_8nGTw	mahmoud arafat	ماذا جرى لمصر؟..التحرش الجنسي. [What happened to Egypt? . . . Sexual harassment]	442
10.	FTxYkb0aBkE	عبدالعزيز السعيدي	التحرش الجنسي في السعودية الصورة الكاملة [Sexual harassment in Saudi Arabia: The full picture]	442

Data retrieved from YouTube May 29, 2017.

officers standing by as sexual harassment takes place. Similarly, the most commented-on video is posted by Fahad Sal, who also has a Saudi talk show. This video is about an incident of sexual harassment that occurred in Jeddah, Saudi Arabia. Two young Saudi girls wearing niqab get sexually harassed by a group of young men, and the poster passionately describes the incident as "awful" as the harassers shout and look like "animals surrounding their prey." The poster mentions the need to have a clear jurisdiction that prohibits and penalizes sexual harassment in Saudi Arabia to eradicate this antisocial phenomenon.

The fifth most-viewed video is entitled "Selma film on sexual harassment." In the tag section, the video is described as a "short drama adapted from real events. A story that happens frequently but the results and outcomes might differ. It's a story of a lady that gets sexually harassed by a co-worker, but Selma refuses and does not surrender. Will she succeed or fail?" The video is produced by "Settat" ("ladies" in Egyptian dialect) on Chat media production, which deals with different issues and concerns that Egyptian women face in their daily lives (see Table 6.2 on page 100). In this video, the producer discusses the goal of making the film in hopes of "enhancing the values of respecting women and knowing her humane and psychological nature. . . . When the stereotypical view of women changes, men can view women in a respectable manner that is fitting with human beings' dignity and high status, especially related to women." The video production discusses the way female workers suffer from sexual advances at the workplace, but in the end no solutions are provided. The video narrates the story of Selma, an unveiled Egyptian woman who is married but whose husband lives abroad. She is continuously harassed by a male co-worker, who wants to take advantage of Selma's vulnerable situation since her husband is abroad and cannot provide protection. Selma protests to her employer but cannot achieve any gains because the harasser tells a completely different version of events to his male employer, who ends up taking no action. The video ends with Selma crying, while her harasser approaches, saying: "Let your honor benefit you." As stated at the beginning of the video, this incident appears to be a common practice occurring at work settings in Egypt, as there is general inaction toward or mistrust of women's complaints of sexual harassment. Testimonies of non-actors are shown at the end of the video, wherein men mostly mention that the fault lies with women who go outside and work without a veil, while veiled women stress that they get sexually harassed everyday upon leaving their homes.

Table 6.2. Social Networking Sites Cited in the Chapter

SNS	Likes/ views/followers	Link
Settat	3.7m	www.youtube.com/user/settatonchat/videos
KAFA	121K	www.facebook.com/kafa.lb
HarassMap	65K	www.facebook.com/HarassMapEgypt
Nefsy	6K	www.facebook.com/-نفسي-مبادرة-ضد-التحرش-الجنسي 272851439480082
Tuskuteesh	30K	www.facebook.com/tuskuteesh
Your Silence Will Not Stop Violence	125K	www.youtube.com/watch?v=XUDYxASzybo

Data collected July 15, 2017.

The final statement is uttered by a sad-looking Egyptian woman, who says: "I wish I was not born a girl." I argue here that though the video refers to workplace sexual harassment, similar behavior is widespread in diverse settings in the Arab world. The film sends a negative message, as it does not end with a hopeful tone or offer any practical solutions to this epidemic cultural problem.

The sixth most-viewed clip deals with a video posted by (www.e3lamak.tv), which is a Public Service Broadcast initiative supported by Belail, a media production company. The video is a social experiment wherein an Egyptian man wears women's make-up and dress, pretending to be a woman to explore her experience on the streets of Cairo. A great deal of cat calling and sexual harassment occurs, and the actor sums up his experience by emphasizing the tremendous difficulties women face simply by walking alone on the streets and that doing so requires significant courage.

Finally, the fourth most commented-on video is from a Moroccan TV show, "Generation News," aired on Medi1TV. One of the guests, Ilyass Lakhrissi, cynically refers to a famous popular saying in Morocco: "If a girl wears what she likes considering it personal freedom, then sexual harassment [by men] becomes a national duty." The main point of the video is to show the patriarchal nature of Moroccan society, where women must abide by males' demands for certain types of dress to avoid being harassed on the streets.

In terms of analysis of YouTube comments, the other most recurrent phrase concerns a Quranic verse (Al Ahzab, 59): "O Prophet, inform thy wives, daughters, and female believers to wear long garments to be recognized and not harmed." The reason for using this verse is to show negative sentiments and opposition toward those who defend women's freedom to wear what they want. Indeed, the verse is meant to offer legitimacy to the above claim because Muslims do not normally argue with or debate "God's spoken words." Yet this verse refers to a pre-Islamic practice, stipulating that "free" women should wear long or full-covering clothes to distinguish themselves from enslaved females who walked the streets without a veil. The custom was meant to help men avoid mistaking "free" women from enslaved women. In fact, this cultural practice dates back to Assyrian times, and was later borrowed by the Greeks and Romans (Brooks, 1923; Heath, 2008; Jastrow, 1921; Llewellyn-Jones, 2007; Olson, 2012), though, ironically, in many Western public debates, the veil is associated with Islam.

Another recurrent statement by YouTube commentators also indicates opposition toward women's freedom. It includes a verse from the Quran, stating, "Settle at your home and do not reveal your attractiveness like those before you in Al Jahiliyah [Pre-Islamic times]" (Al Ahzab, 33). Again, this verse can be misleading, as it deals with instructions given to the prophet Muhammed's wives rather than to all Muslim women.

Finally, another recurring phrase among YouTube commentators involves a saying attributed to Muhammed: "Allah curses men who dress like women," which is used to criticize the video of the Egyptian man who pretended to be a woman, detonating the traditional and conservative values they hold. Once again, commentators often use excerpts from Islamic texts to support their antagonistic views against women, and the general sentiments of their comments are negative toward issues concerning women's freedom. YouTube is used to document cases of sexual harassment and raise awareness to the impact harassment leaves on female victims, yet the online community formed around these videos is not always in agreement, as hostile views frequently dominate discussion online. This is similar to our findings in Chapter 4 on the nature of online communities that gather around women's social movements. All in all, the affordances of social media are manifested in the way likeminded community members can exchange views, describe similar experiences, and receive possible social support in their cultural activism efforts.

Anti-Violence and Sexual Harassment Campaigns

In Chapter 5 we looked at the role of major women's organizations in broadening goals in social activism. Here in this section our focus is on the cultural productions of civil society and grassroots groups that are actively involved in raising awareness about sexual harassment and violence against women. This includes the activities of KAFA (كفى), an Arabic word for "enough." This Lebanese NGO, which stands for "Enough Violence and Exploitation," was established in 2005 (www.kafa.org.lb) and describes itself this way:

> A feminist, secular . . . non-profit, non-governmental civil society organization seeking to create a society that

> is free of social, economic and legal patriarchal structures that discriminate against women. KAFA has been aiming to eliminate all forms of gender-based violence and exploitation since its establishment. . . . It seeks to realize substantive gender equality through the adoption of a combination of different approaches, such as: Advocacy for law reform and introduction of new laws and policies; influencing public opinion, practices and mentality; conducting research and training; and empowering women and children victims of violence, and providing them with social, legal, and psychological support.

This NGO, supported by several international humanitarian organizations and associations, runs campaigns focused on women's human rights and equality, with an emphasis on Lebanon, though it does refer to other Arab countries in its posts. In general, KAFA's campaigns include some that raise awareness on combating prostitution and defending the rights of foreign domestic female workers. For example, the NGO is responsible for disseminating certain hashtags, such as "#Patience has limits," used primarily to criticize judicial rulings in Lebanon that forgive husbands for killing their wives after serving short sentences. The NGO organizes offline protests and asks its members to carry small posters that often include feminist statements such as "masculinity leads to lethal and dangerous judgments." One image retrieved from KAFA's Facebook page states, "The law of my grandfather's time cannot be taken seriously." This campaign is part of KAFA's cultural activism efforts to change the minimum marriage age in Lebanon, and has been launched in coordination with UNFPA and the Norwegian People's Aid. The small girl's braids look like a woman's uterus and are connected to a long gray moustache symbolizing old age and patriarchy. The accompanying text suggests that the law of earlier times does not apply today because it is outdated, as the average age for marriage in Lebanon is currently 16 years for most religious sects. The statement plays on a pun with the word "Jadi" (grandfather and serious), stating, "The law of my grandfather's time cannot be serious."

Some of KAFA's most popular Facebook posts deal with an incident of grave domestic violence committed by a man against his wife in Lebanon, while another addresses the news story of the murder of a married woman (Majida) by her husband. The Facebook post reads:

> Majida is in the coffin because of her murderous husband, Safi Azzelddine, who stabbed her with a knife on Monday at dawn. Safi is married to more than a woman because he simply can. Due to his feelings that he has rights and masculine privileges, he felt that he has the right to end his wife's life similar to tens of other men like him before. Farewell thy woman whose only guilt was to be born a woman on this planet.

The second NGO we will look at in this chapter is Haraas Map (خريطة التحرش الجنسي) (harassmap.org), whose cultural activism effort is focused on sexual harassment in Egypt (Bernardi, 2017). Based on its description, it is "an award-winning volunteer-based initiative founded in late 2010 . . . based on the idea that if more people start taking action when sexual harassment happens in their presence, we can end this epidemic." In other words, the NGO encourages women and bystanders to share information about sexual harassment they experience or witness by directly reporting it. HarassMap offers an interactive map to allow people to view the frequency and locations of sexual harassment in Egypt, relying on the collective and connective efforts of people to succeed: "By taking a collective stand against sexual harassment, we as a society can create social and legal consequences that discourage harassing behaviour and seriously reduce it." The NGO partners with the British Council, Uber, and the Canadian International Development Research center. Regarding Uber, the company trains taxi drivers on sexual harassment and offers them a certificate to ensure that women feel safe when using the service. It is important to note here that sexual harassment in Egypt has garnered international attention, especially during and after the Arab Spring events, for numerous Egyptian and foreign women were sexually assaulted in the streets by groups of men during the popular protests that led to the overthrow of Hosni Mubarak in February 2011 (Amnesty International, 2015; Kingsley, 2013). Also, HarassMap lists 17 types of sexual harassment on its website, including ogling, facial expressions, catcalls, stalking, touching, and others (Harass Map, 2014). In one of its reports, HarassMap notes that 95.3% of female respondents reported having been harassed sometime in the past, while 81.4% of sexual harassment occurs in the streets, in comparison to 14.8% on public transport (Harass Map, 2014).

Online engagement on the organization's Facebook page is relatively limited, despite the fact that the page's organizers frequently urge their audience to interact on the platform by asking them questions and encouraging them to volunteer with the NGO. Based on an examination of the geographical locations of its page followers, the majority are located in Egypt, revealing the national scope of the organization, though some followers are from other Arab countries. As for audience engagement, the second most-liked post is a picture, a cultural production that consists of a series of eight rhetorical questions that aim at discrediting the various harassers' claims and justifications:

1. If harassment is due to poverty, why does the company's manager sexually harass?
2. If harassment is due to late marriage, why does a father sexually harass?
3. If harassment is due to illiteracy, why does a teacher sexually harass?
4. If harassment is due to sexual repression, why does a 7 year old boy sexually harass?
5. If harassment is due to a woman's beautiful body, why do they sexually harass children?
6. If harassment is due to lack of security, why does a police officer sexually harass?
7. If harassment is due to women's attire, why do they sexually harass women wearing niqab?
8. If harassment disappears by ignoring it, why hasn't it disappeared after years of silence?

The message ends with a plea to report the occurrence and location of incidents of sexual harassment, stating: "Your reports will discredit their claims and convince people to thwart harassers." There are, of course, tens, if not hundreds, of other social media campaigns that are more focused on certain countries, such as Nefsy ("I wish") in Egypt,[3] Tuskuteesh ("Don't be silent") in Palestine, and a few others in Saudi

Arabia, some of which will be discussed below.[4] Various forms of cultural productions are used to enhance the cultural activism surrounding the issues of violence and harassment against women in pursuits to create positive change.

In Saudi Arabia, domestic violence against females is believed to be widespread, affecting 87.6% of women and 45% of children (Al Arabiya, 2013). Many Saudi women are subjected to multiple types of domestic abuse, which has been documented by many media outlets (see for example MBC, 2013); one of the most notorious cases receiving wide media attention involved the rape, torture, and murder of Luma Al Ghamdi, a 5-year-old girl. Her attacker was her father, Fayhan Al Ghamdi, a well-known preacher. The judge's decision to free Al Ghamdi in return for blood money created a tremendous uproar (Abdulrahman, 2012; Hall, 2013). This incident prompted the famous Saudi cleric Muhammed Al-Arifi to issue a controversial fatwah on the necessity of having other family members available when fathers stay with their daughters in the same place (Al-Ittihiad, 2012).

Among the popular Saudi social media campaigns combatting domestic violence is "What is hidden is worse: Together to fight violence against women," launched by the King Khalid Philanthropy Foundation in 2013 to raise awareness about violence against women (Al-Khazrami, 2013). It was considered to be the first anti-violence campaign in Saudi Arabia, and the platform used was primarily Twitter, as Saudis are extremely active on Twitter. According to Princess Bandari of the King Khalid Foundation, the campaign's goal is to initiate a discussion on this cultural issue, "as debates can lead to action. We want the society to realize that violence is not acceptable. There is awareness, but what can be done if one witnesses it? How to deal with it?" (Middle East Online, 2013). One image from the campaign shows a woman wearing niqab that reveals only her eyes, one of which has been blackened. With the woman's eyes the only parts shown, the campaign's slogan states: "What is hidden is worse."

Another Saudi initiative is the "White Ribbon" global campaign, which launched its Arabic version in Saudi Arabia in 2013. Abdullah Al Alami, a Saudi male activist residing in Bahrain, created a Facebook page called "No to violence against women and children." The campaign was inspired by previous efforts from female Saudi activists, such as Samar Fattani, who once wrote an article to defend women's causes; the article received two main types of reactions: avid supporters who cite Islamic texts to back their claims, and another group that completely opposes any freedom for women, citing different religious texts (Al Jayoush, 2015). In general, the White Ribbon campaign received encouragement from many Saudis, but it was also rejected within conservative circles. For example, the General Secretary for Muslim Scholars in Saudi Arabia, Nasser Bin Salman Al Omar, criticized the White Ribbon campaign (Kashqari, 2013), stating, "These Westernized initiatives that recently increased are meant to refute the foundations on which this country was established, namely monotheism. . . . We warn that these ideas can introduce malice and endanger the security and safety of this country" (Islamyat, 2013). It is obvious that some clerics in Saudi Arabia feel threatened and concerned that their religious authority and power might be questioned or weakened due to the growing demands for women's rights. To refute women's claims, attacks often cite religious texts and the alleged agenda of Western organizations that are perceived to "corrupt" the pure teachings of Wahhabi Islam in Saudi Arabia.[5]

In conclusion, the influence of social media and its affordances on raising awareness about women's issues, as well as connecting likeminded people and organizations together, are instrumental in the success of these cultural activism campaigns, and various cultural productions are used to achieve these activist goals. Clearly, interest in women's rights is growing not only at the local level but also regionally, though conservative voices remain active in fighting to maintain their power by exploiting certain religious rules and texts. Generally speaking, the interest in women's freedom and equality is shared not only among Arab women, as many men are instrumental in this struggle. The efforts, initiatives, and campaigns discussed above could not have become known and effective without the use of social media, while the influence of globalization, also enhanced by social media, is another factor in promoting cultural activism and the dissemination of information in these anti-violence and sexual harassment campaigns. Indeed, many international humanitarian organizations, especially UN Women, have provided support and guidance to national as well as regional women NGOs in the Arab world to combat injustice. However, cultural change ultimately comes from within the societies that suffer most from gender inequality. The transnational #MeToo Twitter movement has inspired human rights activists and feminists to launch their own online protest—#Masaktach (I won't be silent)—in Morocco, regarding the gang rape of Khadija, a young Moroccan woman (Brémond et al., 2018), as well as a campaign called #MosqueMeToo. Regarding the latter Twitter campaign, some Muslim women from around the world who were sexually harassed during the holy pilgrimage season in Mecca took to social media to raise awareness about this cultural issue, connect with other victims, and speak out to highlight the injustice and harassment in Saudi Arabia and elsewhere in the Muslim world (BBC News, 2018a; Itahawy, 2018).

Conclusion

Due to the influence of local cultural values, which cannot be solely attributed to religious beliefs, nearly all Arab countries are conservative and patriarchal (relatively possible exceptions being Tunisia and Lebanon, though one might argue that all cultures are patriarchal, including Western ones), societies wherein men take major roles in politics and other fields. As a result, women face tremendous challenges in their lives concerning such issues as underage marriage, domestic abuse, and sexual harassment, especially in poor countries or those such as Syria that have experienced armed conflicts. In such a context, feminist issues like women's equality and freedom become highly relevant in this globalized world, and the goal of this book has been to map as well as empirically investigate the way women in the Arab world use new media technologies to positively influence their lives and facilitate change. The convergence of technologies like mobile apps and the affordances of social media have assisted people in general and women in particular as part of globalization from beyond. Yet, the opposing cultural forces that resist women's freedom continue to exert great influence, evident both on the streets and in the widespread practice of sextortion, trolling, and flaming within the online sphere.

This book investigates the use of new media technologies and various forms of activism, including religious, political, social, and cultural activism practiced by diverse female actors and women's organizations. In addition to providing a sociopolitical and historical context of women's issues in the Arab world, the first chapter examines the impact of globalization and convergence in the use of new media technologies in the Arab region. This is followed by a discussion of the theory of (online) influentials in Chapter 2, in connection with the activities of a number of famous female activists. Social media have provided vital new expression venues for well-known women such as Tawakul Karman, Ahlam Mosteghanemi, Nawal El Saadawi, and Nadia Murad, recognized as online influentials or opinion leaders partly because they had offline fame beforehand (Katz & Lazarsfeld, 1955). New media technologies have further empowered such women, and countless others, in the way they connect with their followers, exchange views, voice their social concerns, and broaden their networks. Though leaders often have diverse goals that are limited and oriented in various ways, they all strive to create change in cultural values, and sometimes in politics.

Similar to the argument on female influentials and social media use, Chapter 3 examines how new media technologies have assisted online Muslim communities in spreading their religious beliefs, expressing views, and enhancing their networks. Islamic feminism is comprised of a spectrum of communities including niqabis, hijabis, and unveiled Muslim women who all believe that Islam defines their religious identity, though they express it in different ways. Building on the theory of online religion (Campbell, 2012), online activities are considered part of offline religious beliefs, as a wide array of Muslim online communities practice different types of religious activism. Indeed, there is nothing homogenous about this kind of activism, as the online public sphere itself is segregated along ideological divides; each online religious group is made up of likeminded followers and activists, promoting a diversity of religious values.

Another aspect of the use of new media technologies is manifested in political activism, as Chapter 4 argues that women have become further empowered to voice concerns and assert political demands and rights through the emergence of new media technologies. Resource mobilization theory (McAdam et al., 1996) emphasizes that favorable circumstances are often necessary to pave the way for collective action, and in this instance the favorable circumstance were the events occurring during and following the Arab Spring. Female political activists have since formed a number of important social movements—such as Girls' Revolution and the Uprising of Women in the Arab World—which often gain a following across many Arab countries, and have succeeded in expressing their dissatisfaction with the political reality, especially surrounding the issues of unemployment, corruption, and human rights. Similar to the arguments made on the existence of separate online communities in connection to religious activism, there are three main groups that often interact amongst themselves, such as those that occupy the hegemonic position, oppositional code, and an anti-Islamic but prosocial group (Hall, 2001). In other words, there are clear public "sphericules" (Gitlin, 1998) within the numerous separate online communities.

The existence of these various online communities can be particularly beneficial for women from different Arab countries who have diverse backgrounds, circumstances, beliefs, and subsequently needs. This is further manifested in the discussion in Chapter 5 on social activism and the use of new media technologies, as women's NGOs facilitate the formation of such online communities. They generally function as safe spaces whose goal is to raise awareness, shape the public agenda around urgent issues, and possibly create change. These online spaces and communities can also provide emotional and psychological support through ties established with friends and allies (Furstenberg & Hughes, 1995; Wellman & Wortley, 1990). The efforts of Nasawyia, ABAAD, and IWR, as well as dozens of other NGOs, have direct impact on women's lives, and sometimes on state policies and legislation, such as in the case of changing underage marriage laws in Lebanon and elsewhere. Indeed, social media affordances have generally provided tools for enhanced communication, interaction, and online community building (Halpern & Gibbs, 2013; Meng et al., 2017), and cultural activism, as discussed in Chapter 6, has benefited from these affordances. Many cultural productions such as images and videos posted on social media by individual users, media companies, and official bodies have gone viral and created more cultural awareness regarding issues of domestic violence and sexual harassment against women. As a result, online and offline debates are initiated about these important issues, though it remains unclear whether long-term impact will occur or not.

In my personal view, the future of women activism in the Arab region is promising. As mentioned, numerous forces continue to oppose women's equal rights and emancipation, including the majority of religious authorities and conservative voices who feel that their authority, control, and power are threatened by women's freedom. This resistance or opposing force may differ in its intensity depending on time and context, but positive change in women's lives will occur for many reasons, even if the pace is slow. First and most importantly, public awareness is growing about issues of women's freedom and equal rights, which cannot be silenced or ignored. This is connected to the recent higher literacy rates, enhanced educational levels, and more economic independence among women in comparison to their conditions before the mid–20th century, which certainly enhance their agency, power, and belief that they can make a difference in their lives. Second, the Arab world cannot be disconnected from the rest of the world, as globalization and convergence will continue to play a role in bringing countries together. Also, the ongoing introduction of new mobile technologies, coupled with higher literacies, will open doors for women to express their views, connect with likeminded others, share information, and possibly mobilize themselves. State censorship, no matter how thorough and strict, cannot block these new technologies because there will always be new emerging ones. Finally, Arab men are also increasingly becoming involved in feminist causes for various reasons, including the influence of the diaspora on those living inside the region. Indeed, social progress in women's issues requires collaborative efforts from men and women, while state policies and religious circles must also be supportive of these goals. After all, this progress must come from within the local cultures to sustain and develop, as international pressure might not always be effective, or might sometimes have short-term impact, or be interpreted as part of Western hegemonic efforts to influence the region. For instance, the Saudi government suspended trade with Canada and expelled the Canadian Ambassador in early August 2018, allegedly because of the Canadian government's criticism of the imprisonment of female Saudi activists. The Saudi government regarded this as interference in its internal polices and accused the activists of being supported by foreign powers to undermine their cause. The Saudi reaction is meant to send a warning to other Western countries that they can be economically and possibly politically affected if they think of criticizing, or even referencing, the Saudi human rights record. All of this is part of the forces that resist political and social change in the Kingdom that brands itself as implementing progressive polices to the outside world while remaining regressive toward women's issues.

After all, Arab women are not the focal point here, as they are used as playing cards by officials from different countries to economically pressure each other and/or possibly change state policies. Canada, for example, sold weapons to Saudi Arabia that were periodically used to attack the Houthi rebels in Yemen, but no public condemnations of the use of these weapons have been made. As stated in Chapter 1, some

Western organizations, feminists, and countries adopt a "rescue mission policy" that gives them a sense of moral superiority and license to intervene in the cultural values of others, often without consulting the indigenous members of the culture, including their women. In the West, this argument typically applies to the issue of women's veiling, as debates are not really about the veil and the alleged persecution of women in Islam, but rather about broader internal issues related to racism, xenophobia, and anti-immigration policies. In Canada, for example, Isabelle Charest, Quebec's Status of Women Minister, announced in early 2019 that the veil is a symbol of oppression, a statement that coincided with the province's proposed secularism legislation that aims at prohibiting public servants from wearing religious symbols such as the hijab (Canadian Press, 2019). Yet, these debates occurred when Quebec's National Assembly once had a 30-foot crucifix hanging in its main hall, which Premier François Legault said should remain because it was a "nonreligious symbol" that represents Quebec's history (CBC News, 2019). This kind of double standard reveals issues that have no link to the veil itself but are more related to implicit and explicit hostility toward immigrants and other groups that do not belong in the mainstream dominant culture.

As for limitations of the present study, there are many, as is true for most research. First, large-scope cross-national surveys and/or questionnaires on Arab women's use of social media, which could have provided insight into the affordances of social media in different Arab countries, are missing here. Also, semi-structured interviews with women leaders and online influentials could have offered a better background context for the study, while additional interviews with Arab officials could have provided further information about state policies and plans to combat gender inequality and human rights abuses in various Arab countries.

Future research on women's activism needs to take into account other under-researched platforms, such as closed Facebook Group pages and forums as well as virtual communities like Telegram and WhatsApp, available on some mobile apps. Here, ethnographic research is needed to understand the type of discussions that take place on these outlets and the affordances of new media technologies. Also, differences in ethnic and religious identities among Arab women must be further explored to understand how they are manifested in online and offline discussions. More importantly, large segments of women in the Arab world, such as those living in rural and remote areas, have only partial or sometimes no access to new media technologies, as result of illiteracy, cultural taboos, or insufficient economic means, so it becomes imperative to understand how to introduce these technologies to all individuals in the hopes of positively influencing more lives.

Notes

Chapter 1

1. Also, the Saudi-run MBC channel ran a campaign in 2016 called "#Be free," and its sister channel MBC4 tweeted: "Be free, in your choices, feelings, and life, and don't care about anyone because you're the essence of life" (HuffPost: Arabi, 2017a). Yet the channel was forced to fire three employees, including its social media director on April 5, 2016, two days after launching the campaign due to online criticism from the public (HuffPost: Arabi, 2017b). In fact, the Saudi Prince Abdul Amir Bin Fahad vowed "to destroy" the person responsible for spreading the hashtag, considering it "corruption of religion." Other users called for boycotting the companies that advertise on the channel (Al-Turki, 2017). In a subsequent press release issued by MBC, the channel apologized and mentioned that "one of its staff members who worked in the New Media Department took the initiative of changing the original trajectories of the campaign and launching other platforms/posts that were not part of its core message. . . . The channel pledges that such mistakes will not be repeated in the future." Since MBC is run by Saudi Arabia, including some connections to the royal family (al-Rawi, 2017a), it cannot object to the decisions taken by its sponsors and financial backers.

2. There is gender imbalance in social media use in the MENA region: For every three male Facebook and Twitter users, there is one female user, while LinkedIn has the lowest percentage of women users in the region (Arab Social Media Report, 2017). The percentage of Facebook female users is still lower than the global average, with only 32.3% women users in the MENA region. As for specific countries, Facebook users in Palestine, Twitter in Bahrain, and LinkedIn in Lebanon have the best gender balance in the region, while Facebook users in Oman, Twitter in Yemen, and LinkedIn in Saudi Arabia have the worst (Arab Social Media Report, 2017).

3. Saudi Arabia, for example, ranks first in the Arab world in terms of YouTube viewership, but it also ranks as the "highest YouTube watch time per

capita of any country in the world," according to Tubular Labs (Britton, 2017). This can be explained by the fact that the online platform is regarded as an alternative media outlet that offers ordinary Saudi citizens a venue to express personal views without censorship. Besides, movie theaters, until recently, were banned in the Kingdom, making YouTube a favorite site for posting a variety of videos that might empower people, including women. For example, many Saudi female YouTubers such as Hatoon Kadi, Hessa Al Awad, Al-Juhara Sajer, and Njoud al Shammari have become highly popular in Saudi Arabia despite the conservative views regarding women, for "consumption of female-related [online] content in the Kingdom increased by 75% since last year, according to Google" (Britton, 2017).

Chapter 2

1. After the US invasion of Iraq, the US Embassy was asked by the Department of State to collect the names of the top five most influential women in the country, yet the list primarily included government officials such as Wijdan Salim (Minster of Human Rights), Maysoon Al-Damluji (Parliament member), Hanaa Edwar (Amal humanitarian organization), Nada Al-Sudani (Parliament member), and Tayseer Al-Mashadani (Parliament member) (Wikileaks, 2007). The US Embassy notes that there are clear sectarian biases in the selection, while Iraqi women who are believed "to be influential and who routinely meet with high level US officials, were not necessarily perceived as having great influence within Iraq" by the general public. Edwar is probably the most important Iraqi female activist, as she has been involved in women's issues for decades and has been able to stand against the former Prime Minster of Iraq, Nouri Maliki, and publicly denounce the imprisonment and persecution of human rights activists (Damon, 2011).

2. The author's grandfather, professor Habeeb Al-Rawi, participated in 1951 in a public debate with Daoud on the issue of women's rights. Unfortunately, he stated that the timing was not right for granting women full political rights. I personally believe he was mistaken and that he should have supported Daoud's efforts.

3. In terms of Arab women with popular social media channels, Lebanon ranks first among the three main social media platforms—YouTube (n = 3), Facebook (n = 7), and Twitter (n = 8)—followed by Syria on Twitter (n = 4) and YouTube (n = 2), Jordan on Twitter (n = 3) and Facebook (n = 2), and Tunisia and Algeria on Facebook (n = 2). For example, the YouTube channel, SyrianGirlpartisan, ranks number 6 in Syria and is run by a pro-Bashar Assad woman who is fluent in English. She is often interviewed by InfoWars, the infamous far-right website that promotes conspiracy theories. As for Facebook,

the following pages rank in the top 10: "Women of Heaven" (Egypt, no. 5; see Chapter 3); Shatha Hassoun, a singer (Iraq, no. 9); "Libyan Ladies," a women's online community (Libya, no. 4); Khadija Ben Guenna (Saudi Arabia, no. 5); Nimco Dareen, a singer (Somalia, no. 4); and Ahlam (UAE, no. 10) (data compiled and organized by the author from www.socialbakers.com).

4. Facebook data were retrieved on December 29, 2016; Mosteghanemi's 174 Facebook posts from November 14 to December 29, 2016, generated 4,504,914 likes and 254,481 comments.

Chapter 3

1. Similar to the previous online group, "The Righteous Woman" (المرأة الصالحة) is a moderate Muslim women's community created to promote Islamic marriage, with an emphasis on modesty. As the page describes itself, "men and women are tools to establish a good Islamic society due to their offspring; henceforth, they have to choose their life partners based on religious criteria." These criteria are allegedly related to following the teachings of Islam, especially women wearing the veil, hence the group's name "The Righteous Woman." In other words, according to this online community, the "righteous woman" is someone who wears the veil, prays, memorizes the Quran, and follows Islamic teachings. These religious attributes presumably lift the social condition of Muslim women by making them more marriageable. Based on an analysis of the top 10 posts (ranked by number of likes), most statements relate to the importance of marriage and contain happy Muslim wishes such as Islamic prayers and supplications with a clear emphasis on women wearing the veil. Similar to the previous online group, the images retrieved from this page also contain many that imitate the Japanese anime style, possibly for the reasons given above.

2. These online communities are available on various social media outlets, particularly Facebook, which includes "Princess by My Own Morals," "Women of Paradise," "My Beautiful Beloved Is a Muslim," "My Veil Is the Secret of My Beauty," and "Muslim Girl." The founder of the latter page, Amani Al-Khatahtbeh, states that its goal is "to make the conversation about us" in an effort to empower Muslim women (Convery, 2017; *The Guardian*, 2017).

3. Nearly all the images depict white women rather than brown or black females, indirectly suggesting that whiteness is a defining feature of beauty.

4. For example, there are the "With my niqab, I satisfy my God" and "Niqabis." The latter page is created for Moroccan niqabi women, and its description mentions the following brief statement: "I'm a Muslim woman, and I'm not a criminal." Finally, there are also "Niqabi and Proud of it," "Virtuous Niqabis," and "Kingdom of Niqab."

Chapter 4

1. Note that offline feminist movements did exist before the Arab Spring events, but they were limited in scope and influence (for more details, see Abu-Lughod, 1998; El Saadawi, 2007; Sidani, 2005). For example, in November 1990, a group of about 50 Saudi women gathered to protest the driving ban. As punishment, the women's passports were confiscated, and they lost their jobs (Associated Press, 2014; Róisín, 2015).

2. Twitter was chosen because it is regarded as the most active platform in Saudi Arabia, with over 2.4 million users, generating over 40% of all Arabic language tweets (Arab Social Media Report, 2015).

3. In late December 2016, for example, a popular music video was released by Majed Alesa that showcases Saudi women dancing, playing basketball, and skating to mock the macho men culture of Saudi Arabia. Interestingly, US president Donald Trump is repeatedly featured in the video, as a subtle connection is made between his controversial stances and degrading attitudes toward women and the challenges faced by Saudi women (YouTube, 2016).

Chapter 5

1. Some of the early NGOs in Iraq include Women's Revival Club (1923), Women's Rights League (1952), and the Muslim Sisters Association (NCCI, 2011).

2. For example, the sixth most-liked post tells of a Syrian man who plucked out the teeth of his wife of 18 years and fatally stabbed her.

Chapter 6

1. The Yemeni movie production entitled "I am Nojoom" deals with a 10 years old girl called Nojoom (stars) who got married in an early age as there are no laws that prohibit such a practice in Yemen; the film tackles other important issues like domestic abuse and sexual exploitation.

2. This also includes the taboos surrounding the issue of sexually transmitted diseases like HIV (See Al-Rawi, 2017e).

3. This social media campaign was sponsored in part by UN Women "inspired by snowballing social media discussions on sexual harassment in Egypt, and a group of independent activists took the conversation to an offline public. They wanted to organize activities in the public sphere that raised awareness and caused a ripple effect, both by building support against sexual

harassment and creating debate within Egyptian society using the most simple of approaches: the country's first 'human chain' against sexual harassment" (UN Women, 2013b, p. 6). UN Women mentioned that the photos taken of campaign followers went viral, as the "number of fans jumped by 4,000 people; the photo album was viewed by 50,000 Facebook users; and through comments, shares and clicks, it engaged at least 45,000 of them" (UN Women, 2013b, p. 7).

4. The initiative is run by Khulood Khamis, a female activist from Haifa, Palestine, who specializes in assisting victims of sexual assaults. It describes itself as a "safe zone for women to share their stories of sexual harassments and assaults. If you find difficulties in expressing yourself in words, you can post an artistic production, instead."

5. Three other Saudi grassroots campaigns are relevant here. The first one is called "1919 Life" (www.1919.life), an interactive campaign that is part of the Al Waleed Philanthropic organization. The interactive quality of this awareness campaign is interesting because it indirectly shows how violence against women takes place. One image, for example, shows a bruised woman with the following written statement: "Your silence is an indication of approval. Share with us to raise awareness." The second campaign, launched primarily on Twitter, is called "#Beat her" and produced by Libra Productions. The organizers asked ordinary male and female Saudis to share their ideas regarding the beating of women, and about 252 Saudis volunteered to be photographed carrying posters. One volunteer stated that "Harem's age has gone! . . . By Allah it hasn't; we are now living in the concubine's age" (CNN Arabic, 2013). The campaign was referenced by the title "The Upraising of Women in the Arab World" on its Facebook page (see Chapter 4), which indicates the kind of close connections these feminist initiatives acquire in the region. Finally, the third campaign is a much smaller one called "Your silence will not stop violence," launched on YouTube, with the primary objective of highlighting the importance of reporting domestic abuse and protecting women from violence.

Works Cited

Abadeer, A. (2015). *Norms and gender discrimination in the Arab world.* New York: Palgrave Macmillan.

Abbas, S. (2012, December 2). Revolution is female: The uprising of women in the Arab world. Open Democracy. Open Democracy. www.opendemocracy.net/5050/sara-abbas/revolution-is-female-uprising-of-women-in-arab-world

Abdel-Nabi, S., Agha, J., Choucair, J., & Mikdashi, M. (2004). Pop goes the Arab world: Popular music, gender, politics, and transnationalism in the Arab world. *Hawwa*, *2*(2), 231–254.

Abdulrahman, A. (2012, December 18). Violence against Women: What is hidden is worse. *Okaz* newspaper. Retrieved from okaz.com.sa/article/529063

Abdulhakim, Mahmood. (2017, August 2). Sexual allusions clips cause their fame. . . . Huffpost—Arabi. Retrieved from www.huffpostarabi.com/2017/08/02/story_n_17654964.html

Abu-Lughod, L. (Ed.). (1998). *Remaking women: Feminism and modernity in the Middle East.* Princeton, NJ: Princeton University Press.

Abu-Lughod, L. (2002). Do Muslim women really need saving? Anthropological reflections on cultural relativism and its others. *American Anthropologist*, *104*(3), 783–790.

Abu-Lughod, L. (2013). *Do Muslim women need saving?* Cambridge, MA: Harvard University.

Abu-Lughod, L., & El-Mahdi, R. (2011). Beyond the "woman question" in the Egyptian revolution. *Feminist Studies*, *37*(3), 683–691.

Abu-Odeh, L. (2004). Egyptian feminism: Trapped in the identity debate. *Yale JL & Feminism*, *16*, 145.

Afkhami, M., & Friedl, E. (Eds.). (1997). *Muslim women and the politics of participation: Implementing the Beijing platform.* Syracuse, NY: Syracuse University Press.

AFP. (2016, December 28). Afrah Shawqi: Iraqi journalist kidnapped from Baghdad home. *The Guardian*. Retrieved from www.theguardian.com/world/2016/dec/28/afrah-shawqi-iraqi-journalist-kidnapped-from-baghdad-home

Agarwal, N., Lim, M., and Wigand, R.T. (2015). *Online collective action and the role of social media in mobilizing opinions: A case study on women's right-to-drive campaigns in Saudi Arabia*. Paper presented at the meeting of the twenty-first Americas Conference on Information Systems, Puerto Rico.

Agence France Press. (2016, November 4). Author Leïla Slimani urges Moroccans to rebel against "medieval" laws. *The Guardian*. Retrieved from www.theguardian.com/world/2016/nov/04/author-leila-slimani-moroccans-rebel-against-medieval-laws-human-rights

Ahlammosteghanemi.com. (n.d.). About the author. Retrieved from www.ahlammosteghanemi.com/about

Ahmari, S. (2013, March 22). Manal Al-Sharif: The Woman Who Dared to Drive. *Wall Street Journal*. Retrieved from www.wsj.com/articles/SB10001424127887324077704578362160166544782

Ahmed, L. (1992). *Women and gender in Islam: Historical roots of a modern debate*. New Haven, CT: Yale University Press.

Al Ahram. (2016, February 4). In an MA study, Turkish TV series threaten the fabric of Egyptian families. Retrieved from aitmag.ahram.org.eg/News/42815.aspx

Al Al-Sheikh, A. (2012, January 27). New technologies: Their advantages and disadvantages. Retrieved from 1433-03-04ه- التقنيات-الحديثة-سلبياتها-وإيجابياتها

Al Al-Sheikh, A. (n.d.). The Dangers of satellite channels on people's beliefs. Retrieved from www.mufti.af.org.sa/ar/content خطر-القنوات-الفضائية-على-عقائد-الناس

Al Arabiya. (2010, September 5). Algerian author preaches to women on Facebook. Retrieved from www.alarabiya.net/articles/2010/09/05/118549.html

Al Arabiya. (2013, June 26). Increase in violence against Saudi women reaching 87%. Retrieved from goo.gl/1NxXoE

Al Ghad, A. (2015, December 31). A GCC citizen blackmails Saudi women who are alluded with "WhosHere." Retrieved from m.adengd.net/news/187064

Al Haj, A. (2017, February 1). Intellectual liberation. Nasawiya. Retrieved from nasawyia.org/2017/02/01/التحرر-الفكري

Al Hurra. (2017, May 18). She's 27 years old. . . . First Iraqi woman flying a Boeing. Retrieved from www.alhurra.com/a/iraqi-woman-pilot-boing-/365079.html

Al Jayoush, K. (2015, March 22). Men in the forefront in rejecting violence against women. *Al Hayat* newspaper. Retrieved from www.alhayat.com/m/story/8200421#sthash.ceTeNQxf.dpbs

Al Sadawi, N. (2017, February 12). The Saudi Labor Ministry succeeds in locating the husband who abused his wife in the south. *Sayidaty magazine*. Retrieved from goo.gl/S7QTaE

Al Sharabi, M. (2014, December 27). From Imam Ahmed to Tuhfa Hable: The story of the first Yemen woman who leads a demonstration. Al Mashhad Al Yemeni. Retrieved from almashhad-alyemeni.com/news44994.html

Alahmed, A. (2014). The potential of political changes in the Information Age: The political challenges sphere of Saudi Arabia through citizen activism. In A. M. Solo. (Ed.), *Handbook of research on political activism in the Information Age* (pp. 37–59). Hershey, PA: IGI Global.

Al-Ali, N. (2012a). The Iraqi women's movement: Past and contemporary perspectives. In P. Arenfeldt & N. Golley (Eds.). *Mapping Arab women's movements: A century of transformations from within* (pp. 43–64). Cairo: American University of Cairo Press.

Al-Ali, N. (2012b). Gendering the Arab Spring. *Middle East Journal of Culture and Communication*, *5*(1), 26–31.

Al-Awad, B. (2014, December 15). Because of his wife, threats to "harm" Al-Ghamdi. Al-Watan Online. Retrieved from www.alwatan.com.sa/Nation/News_Detail.aspx?ArticleID=208831

Al-Ittihiad. (2012, January 16). Al-Arifi: A girl should not sit along with her father unless her mother is present. Retrieved from www.alittihad.ae/details.php?id=5036&y=2012

Ali, S. 2000. *Gender and human rights in Islam and international law: Equal before Allah, unequal before man?* The Hague: Kluwer Law International.

Alkhalisi, Z. (2017). New app helps Saudi women claim their rights. CNN. Retrieved from money.cnn.com/2017/07/20/technology/saudi-app-women-rights/index.html

Al-Khazrami, A. (2013, April 30). A Twitter campaign to stop violence against Saudi women. Al Yaum. Retrieved from www.alyaum.com/article/3080721

Al-Krenawi, A. (2013). *Psychosocial impact of polygamy in the Middle East*. Springer Science & Business Media.

Al-Malki, A., Kaufer, D., Ishizaki, S., & Dreher, K. (2012). *Arab women in Arab news: Old stereotypes and new media*. New York: Bloomsbury Academic.

Almahasheer, M. B. (2018). Feminism in the works of Fawziyya Abū Khālid. *CLCWeb: Comparative Literature and Culture*, *20*(1), 6.

Al-Olayan, F. S., & Karande, K. (2000). A content analysis of magazine advertisements from the United States and the Arab world. *Journal of Advertising*, *29*(3), 69–82.

Al-Rasheed, M. (2013). *A most masculine state: Gender, politics and religion in Saudi Arabia* (vol. 43). Cambridge: Cambridge University Press.

Al-Rawi, A. (2010). Iraqi women journalists' challenges and predicaments. *Journal of Arab & Muslim Media Research*, *3*(3), 223–236.

Al-Rawi, A. (2014). The Arab Spring and online protests in Iraq. *International Journal of Communication*, *8*(1), 916–942.

Al-Rawi, A. (2014). Framing the online women's movements in the Arab world. *Information, Communication & Society*, *17*(9), 1147–1161.

Al-Rawi, A. (2015). Sectarianism and the Arab Spring: Framing the popular protests in Bahrain. *Global Media and Communication, 11*(1), 25–42.

Al-Rawi, A. (2016). Understanding the social media audiences of radio stations. *Journal of Radio & Audio Media, 23*(1), 50–67.

Al-Rawi, A. (2017a). Assessing public sentiments and news preferences on Al Jazeera and Al Arabiya. *International Communication Gazette, 79*(1), 1–32.

Al-Rawi, A. (2017b). Online political activism in Syria: Sentiment analysis of social media. *Sage Research Studies Cases*, 1–25.

Al-Rawi, A. (2017c). Facebook and virtual nationhood: Social media and the Arab Canadians community. *AI & Society*, 1–13.

Al-Rawi, A. (2017d). News organizations 2.0: A comparative study of Twitter news. *Journalism Practice, 11*(6), 705–720.

Al-Rawi, A. (2017e). Exploring HIV-AIDS interests in the MENA region using internet-based searches. *First Monday, 22*(10).

Al-Rawi, A., & Fahmy, S. (2018). Social media use in the diaspora: The case of Syrians in Italy. In K. Karim & A. Al-Rawi (Eds.). *Diaspora and media in Europe: Migration, identity, and integration* (pp. 71–96). London: Palgrave Macmillan.

Al-Rawi, K. (2010). *The history of the press and media in Iraq* (in Arabic). Damascus: Dar Safahat.

Al-Samarai, I. (2016). Blocking internet website's that threaten the security and social conditions. Iraqi Media Network. Retrieved from www.imn.iq/archives/2514

Al-Sarai, A. (2012, November 18). An Iraqi girl revolts against a patriarchal society. *Al-Hayat* newspaper.

Alsharif, A. (2012, April 4). Taboo-breaking Saudi films spur debate in staid kingdom. Reuters. Retrieved from www.reuters.com/article/entertainment-us-saudi-online-taboo/taboo-breaking-saudi-films-spur-debate-in-staid-kingdom-idUSBRE8330RW20120404

Al-Sharif, M. (2017). *Daring to drive: A Saudi woman's awakening*. New York: Simon & Schuster.

Alter, C. (2015, December 20). A Yezidi woman who escaped ISIS slavery tells her story. *Time*. Retrieved from time.com/4152127/isis-yezidi-woman-slavery-united-nations

Al-Turki, W. (2016, October 26). Popular Saudi dismay against the *New York Times*: This is the story of women featured in a film that is received with anger. *Huffington Post Arabi*. Retrieved from www.huffpostarabi.com/2016/10/26/story_n_12652258.html

Al-Turki, W. (2017, April 4). #Be Free: Alert at MBC group after the threat of a Saudi prince to destroy it due to a hashtag. HuffPost—Arabi. Retrieved from www.huffpostarabi.com/2017/04/03/story_n_15783452.html?utm_hp_ref=arabi

Amin, H. (2002). Freedom as a value in Arab media: Perceptions and attitudes among journalists. *Political Communication, 19*(2), 125–135.

Amnesty International. (2015). "Circles of hell": Domestic, public and state violence against women in Egypt. Retrieved from www.amnestyusa.org/files/mde_120042015.pdf

Amnesty International. (2016). End the horror in Syria's torture prisons. Retrieved from www.amnesty.org/en/latest/campaigns/2016/08/syria-torture-prisons

Amnesty International. (2017, June 5). Saudi Arabia detains rights activist who defied women's driving ban. Retrieved from www.amnesty.org/en/latest/news/2017/06/saudi-arabia-detains-rights-activist-who-defied-womens-driving-ban

Amos, D. (2018). Arrests of Saudi women's rights activists "point to the limits of change." NPR. Retrieved from www.npr.org/sections/parallels/2018/05/22/613040254/arrests-of-saudi-womens-rights-activists-point-to-the-limits-of-change

Appadurai, A. (1996). *Modernity at large: Cultural dimensions of globalization.* Minneapolis: University of Minnesota Press.

Arab.org. (n.d.). NGO Portal: Countries. Retrieved from arab.org/countries

Arab Social Media Report. (2011). The role of social media in Arab women's empowerment. Retrieved from www.arabsocialmediareport.com/UserManagement/PDF/ASMR%20Report%203.pdf

Arab Social Media Report. (2015). Twitter in the Arab region. Retrieved from www.arabsocialmediareport.com/Twitter/LineChart.aspx?&PriMenuID=18&CatID=25&mnu=Cat

Arab Social Media Report. (2017). Social media and the internet of things: Towards data-driven policymaking in the Arab world: Potential, limits and concerns. Retrieved from www.mbrsg.ae/getattachment/1383b88a-6eb9-476a-bae4-61903688099b/Arab-Social-Media-Report-2017

Arberry, A. (1955). *The Koran interpreted.* London: Allen & Unwin.

Associated Press. (2013, May 29). Femen topless protest targets Tunisia's justice ministry. *The Guardian.* Retrieved from www.theguardian.com/world/2013/may/29/tunisia-femen-protest-amina-tyler

Associated Press. (2014, December 25). Two women referred to "terror" court for driving in Saudi Arabia. *The Guardian.* Retrieved from www.theguardian.com/world/2014/dec/25/women-charged-saudi-arabia-driving-ban-terror-court

Auger, G. (2013). Fostering democracy through social media: Evaluating diametrically opposed nonprofit advocacy organizations' use of Facebook, Twitter, and YouTube. *Public Relations Review, 39*(4), 369–376.

Badran, M. (2013). *Feminism in Islam: Secular and religious convergences.* New York: Oneworld Publications.

Bager, J. (2015, February 6). Saudi women right-to-drive activists deploy Twitter, face terrorism court. *Time*. Retrieved from time.com/3697073/saudi-arabia-women-drive-twitter

Bakshy E., Hofman J., Mason W., et al. (2011) Everyone's an Influencer: Quantifying influence on Twitter. *Proceedings of the Fourth ACM International Conference on Web Search and Data Mining.* Hong Kong, China: ACM, 65–74.

Baljon, J. (1994). Indian Muftīs and the prohibition of images. *Islamic studies, 33*(4), 479–484.

Bastos, M. T., & Mercea, D. (2016). Serial activists: Political Twitter beyond influentials and the Twittertariat. *New Media & Society, 18*(10), 2359–2378.

Baym, N. K. (2000). *Tune in, log on: Soaps, fandom, and online community* (vol. 3). Thousand Oaks, CA: Sage.

BBC News. (2016a, October 26). Sex, honour, shame and blackmail in an online world. BBC News. Retrieved from www.bbc.com/news/magazine-37735368

BBC News. (2016b, December 27). Iraq gunmen kidnap campaigning female journalist. Retrieved from www.bbc.com/news/world-middle-east-38442805

BBC News. (2017, July 30). Maryam al-Otaibi: Saudi anti-guardianship campaigner freed from detention. Retrieved from www.bbc.com/news/world-middle-east-40770776

BBC News. (2017a, August 27). Lebanon rape law: Parliament abolishes marriage loophole. Retrieved from www.bbc.com/news/world-middle-east-40947448

BBC News. (2017b, December 27). #MeToo, #TakeAKnee and #Covfefe: Hashtags that dominated in 2017. Retrieved from www.bbc.com/news/world-42251490

BBC News. (2017c, September 27). Saudi Arabia driving ban on women to be lifted. Retrieved from www.bbc.com/news/world-middle-east-41408195

BBC News. (2018, February 24). "Groped by holy mosque guard during Hajj" in Mecca. Retrieved from www.bbc.com/news/av/world-middle-east-43174322/groped-by-holy-mosque-guard-during-hajj-in-mecca

BBC News. (2018, October1). Former Miss Iraq "threatened" after fellow Instagram star's murder. Retrieved from www.bbc.com/news/world-middle-east-45706227

Bennett, L. (2003). Communicating global activism. *Information, Communication & Society, 6*(2), 143–168.

Bennett, W. L., & Segerberg, A. (2011). Digital media and the personalization of collective action: Social technology and the organization of protests against the global economic crisis. *Information, Communication & Society, 14*(6), 770–799.

Benkler, Y. 2006. *The wealth of networks: How social production transforms markets and freedoms.* New Haven, CT: Yale University Press.

Ben Moussa, M. (2011). The use of the internet by social movements in Morocco: Implications for collective action and political change. Unpublished PhD Dissertation. Concordia University, Canada.

Bernardi, C. (2017). HarassMap: The silent revolution for women's rights in Egypt. In E. Maestri & A. Profanter (Eds.). *Arab women and the media in changing landscapes* (pp. 215–228). London: Palgrave Macmillan.

Bimber, B. (1990). Karl Marx and the three faces of technological determinism. *Social Studies of Science, 20*(2), 333–351.

Biographical Encyclopedia of the Modern Middle East and North Africa. (2008). Mustaghanmi, Ahlam (1953–). Retrieved from www.highbeam.com/doc/1G2-2830800217.html

Bjerke, B., & Al-Meer, A. (1993). Culture's consequences: Management in Saudi Arabia. *Leadership & Organization Development Journal, 14*(2), 30–35.

Borgatti, S. P. (2005). Centrality and network flow. *Social networks, 27*(1), 55–71.

Borge-Holthoefer, J., Rivero, A., García, I., Cauhé, E., Ferrer, A., Ferrer, D., & Sanz, F. (2011). Structural and dynamical patterns on online social networks: The Spanish May 15th movement as a case study. *PloS one, 6*(8), e23883.

Borra, E., & Rieder, B. (2014). Programmed method: Developing a toolset for capturing and analyzing tweets. *Aslib Journal of Information Management, 66*(3), 262–278.

Brecher, J., Costello, T., & Smith, B. (2000). *Globalization from below: The power of solidarity*. Boston: South End Press.

Brémond, A., Baqué, I., Hakimm, S., Spera, C., & Ford, L. (2018, November 26). "I will not keep silent": Khadija rape case spurs women into action in Morocco. Video. *The Guardian*. Retrieved from www.theguardian.com/global-development/video/2018/nov/23/i-will-not-keep-silent-khadija-case-sparks-backlash-in-morocco-video

Britton, B. (2017, April 5). Why women are taking to YouTube in Saudi Arabia. CNN. Retrieved from edition.cnn.com/2017/04/04/middleeast/saudi-arabia-youtube/index.html

Brooks, B. A. (1923). Some observations concerning ancient Mesopotamian women. *The American Journal of Semitic Languages and Literatures, 39*(3), 187–194.

Buffon, V., & Allison, C. (2016). The gendering of victimhood: Western media and the Sinjar genocide. *Kurdish Studies, 4*(2), 176–196.

Burgess, J., & Green, J. 2009. *YouTube: Online Video and Participatory Culture.* Cambridge: Polity Press.

Butler, B. (2001). Membership size, communication activity, and sustainability: A resource-based model of online social structures. *Information Systems Research, 12*(4), 346–362.

Butler, J. (2004). *Undoing gender*. London: Psychology Press.

Butt, R., & Nixon, N. (2008, October 18). US academic first woman to lead Muslim prayers in UK. *The Guardian*. Retrieved from www.theguardian.com/world/2008/oct/18/amina-wadud-mecca-muslims

Calderwood, J. (2011, August 2). MPs attack "offensive" Kuwaiti TV show "High School Girls." *The National*. Retrieved from www.thenational.ae/news/.../mps-attack-offensive-kuwaiti-tv-show-high-school-girls

Calhoun, C. (2004). Information technology and the international public sphere. In D. Schuler & P. Day (Eds.). *Shaping the network society: The new role of civil society in cyberspace* (pp. 229–252). Cambridge, MA: MIT Press.

Calvert, J. (2009). *Sayyid Qutb and the origins of radical Islamism*. London: Hurst & Company Limited.

Campbell, K. E., & Lee, B. A. (1992). Sources of personal neighbor networks: Social integration, need, or time? *Social Forces*, 1077–1100.

Campbell, H. (2012). Understanding the relationship between religion online and offline in a networked society. *Journal of the American Academy of Religion*, *80*(1), 64–93.

Canadian Press. (2019, February 6). Quebec Status of Women Minister Isabelle Charest says Hijab is a symbol of oppression. *Huffington Post*. Retrieved from www.huffingtonpost.ca/2019/02/06/quebec-status-of-women-minister-isabelle-charest-says-hijab-is-a-symbol-of-oppression_a_23663082/

Caren, N., Jowers, K., & Gaby, S. (2012). A social movement online community: Stormfront and the white nationalist movement. *Research in Social Movements, Conflict, and Change*, *33*, 163–193.

Carland, S. (2017). *Fighting Hislam: Women, faith and sexism*. Melbourne: Melbourne University Press.

Carroll, W., & Hacket, R. (2006). Democratic media activism through the lens of social movement theory. *Media, Culture & Society*, *28*(1), 83–104.

Castells, M. (2001). *The internet galaxy*. Oxford: Oxford University Press.

Castells, M. (2007). Communication, power and counter-power in the network society. *International Journal of Communication*, *1*(1), 29.

Castells, M. (2008). The new public sphere: Global civil society, communication networks and global governance. *The Annals of the American Academy of Political and Social Science*, *616*, 78–93.

Castells, M. (2011). *The rise of the network society: The information age: Economy, society, and culture*. New York: John Wiley & Sons.

CBC News. (2019, March 29). Should the crucifix in Quebec's National Assembly come down? Retrieved from www.cbc.ca/news/canada/montreal/should-the-crucifix-in-quebec-s-national-assembly-come-down-1.5076077

Cestor, E. (2010). Music and television in Lebanon. In M. A. Frishkopf (ed.). *Music and media in the Arab world* (pp. 97–110). Cairo: The American University of Cairo.

Cha, M., Haddadi, H., Benevenuto, F., & Gummadi, P. K. (2010). Measuring user influence on Twitter: The million follower fallacy. *ICWSM*, *10*(10–17), 30.

Chadwick, A., & Howard, P. (Eds.). (2009). *Routledge handbook of internet politics*. London: Routledge.

Chang, W. (2005). Online civic participation and political empowerment. *Media, Culture & Society, 27*, 925–935.

Chaudhry, I. (2014). Arab revolutions: Breaking fear|# hashtags for change: Can Twitter generate social progress in Saudi Arabia? *International Journal of Communication, 8*(19).

Cheref, A. (2010). *Gender and identity in North Africa: Postcolonialism and feminism in Maghrebi women's literature* (vol. 94). New York: IB Tauris.

Cheung, C. M., Chiu, P. Y., & Lee, M. K. (2011). Online social networks: Why do students use Facebook?. *Computers in Human Behavior, 27*(4), 1337–1343.

Chittal, N. (2015, March 26). How social media is changing the feminist movement. MSNBC. Retrieved from www.msnbc.com/msnbc/how-social-media-changing-the-feminist-movement

Choi, S. (2015). The two-step flow of communication in Twitter-based public forums. *Social Science Computer Review, 33*(6), 696–711.

CNN Arabic. (2013, 27 June) 27. "#Beat Her": A campaign for Arab men rejecting the punishments of wives. Retrieved from archive.arabic.cnn.com/2013/twitter/5/28/hit.her.campaign

CNN Arabic. (2014a, February 10). Saudi Arabia . . . the man who publicly announced his sins leaves prison as a mosque prayer announcer. Retrieved from arabic.cnn.com/middleeast/2014/02/10/saudi-womanizer-released

CNN Arabic. (2014b, December 15). The consequences of the televised appearance of Sheikh Al-Ghamdi's wife without a niqab continues. . . . Retrieved from arabic.cnn.com/middleeast/2014/12/15/twitter-saudi-ghamdi-interview

Coleman, I. (2011, December 20). Is the Arab Spring bad for women? Overthrowing male dominance could be harder than overthrowing a dictator. *Foreign Policy*. Retrieved from foreignpolicy.com/2011/12/20/is-the-arab-spring-bad-for-women

Convery, S. (2017, August 25). MuslimGirl's Amani Al-Khatahtbeh: "We decided to make the conversation about us." *The Guardian*. Retrieved from www.theguardian.com/culture/2017/aug/25/muslimgirls-amani-al-khatahtbeh-we-decided-to-make-the-conversation-about-us

Conway, M., & McInerney, L. (2008). Jihadi video and auto-radicalisation: Evidence from an exploratory YouTube study. *Intelligence and Security Informatics, 5376*, 108–118.

Cooke, M. (2016). Women and the Arab Spring: A transnational, feminist Revolution. In Fatima Sadiqi (ed.). *Women's movements in post-"Arab Spring" North Africa* (pp. 31–44). New York: Palgrave Macmillan.

Cooke, R. (2015, October 11). Nawal El Saadawi: "Do you feel you are liberated? I feel I am not." *The Guardian*. Retrieved from www.theguardian.com/

books/2015/oct/11/nawal-el-saadawi-interview-do-you-feel-you-are-liberated-not

Cordall, S., & Mahmood, M. (2017, September 4). "We are an example to the Arab world": Tunisia's radical marriage proposals. *The Guardian*. Retrieved from www.theguardian.com/global-development/2017/sep/04/we-are-an-example-to-the-arab-world-tunisias-radical-marriage-proposals

Cunningham, S., Hawkins, G., Yue, A., Nguyen, T., & Sinclair, J. (2000). Multicultural broadcasting and diasporic video as public sphericules. *American Behavioral Scientist, 43*(9), 1533–1547.

Damon, A. (2011, October 6). The woman who lambasted Iraq's prime minister. CNN. Retrieved from www.cnn.com/2011/10/06/world/meast/iraqi-women

Deibert, R. J. (2000). International plug'n play? Citizen activism, the internet, and global public policy. *International Studies Perspectives, 1*(3), 255–272.

Della Porta, D. (Ed.). (2006). *Globalization from below: Transnational activists and protest networks*. Minneapolis: University of Minnesota Press.

Della Porta, D., & Diani, M. (2006). *Social movements: An introduction*. Malden, MA: Blackwell Publishing.

Devi, G. (2015, December 18). Fatima Mernissi obituary. *The Guardian*. Retrieved from www.theguardian.com/world/2015/dec/18/fatima-mernissi-obituary

Dönmez-Colin, G. (2004). *Women, Islam and cinema*. London: Reaktion Books.

Dubai School of Government. (2013). The Arab world online: Trends in internet usage in the Arab region. Retrieved from archives.dimed.gouv.fr/sites/dimed.gouv.fr/files/asmr_-_the_arab_world_online_trends_in_internet_usage_in_the_arab_region_-_avril_2013.pdf

Dubai School of Government. (2014). The Arab world online 2014: Trends in internet and mobile usage in the Arab region. Retrieved from www.mbrsg.ae/getattachment/ff70c2c5-0fce-405d-b23f-93c198d4ca44/The-Arab-World-Online-2014-Trends-in-Internet-and.aspx

Duerden, J. (2018, January 11). "I can't describe my feelings"—Saudi women finally allowed into games. *The Guardian*. Retrieved from www.theguardian.com/football/2018/jan/11/saudi-arabia-women-professional-stadium-fan-al-hilal

Echchaibi, N. (2013). Muslimah media watch: Media activism and Muslim choreographies of social change. *Journalism, 14*(7), 852–867.

The Economist. (2016, September 17). Breaking up in Baghdad: A rise in divorces is blamed on Islamism, poverty and Turkish soap operas. Retrieved from www.economist.com/news/middle-east-and-africa/21707172-rise-divorces-blamed-islamism-poverty-and-turkish-soap-operas-breaking

El Mkaouar, L. (2016). *Power, Arab media moguldum & gender rights as entertainment in the Middle East*. Unpublished doctoral dissertation, University of Westminster.

El Saadawi, N. (2005). Sexual aggression against the female child. In H. Moghissi (Ed.). *Women and Islam: Images and realities* (vol. 1) (pp. 17–20). London: Routledge.

El Saadawi, N. (2007). *The hidden face of Eve: Women in the Arab world*. New York: Zed Books.

El-Naggar, M., & Bolt, A. (2016, October 14). "Ladies First": Saudi Arabia's female candidates. *New York Times*. Retrieved from www.nytimes.com/video/world/middleeast/100000004711633/ladies-first-saudi-arabias-female-candidates.html

El-Nawawy, M., & Khamis, S. (2009). *Islam dot com: Contemporary Islamic discourse in cyberspace*. Hampshire: Palgrave Macmillan.

Eltantawy, N. (2013). From veiling to blogging: Women and media in the Middle East. *Feminist Media Studies, 13*(5), 765–769.

Engineer, A. (2008). *The rights of women in Islam*. New York: Sterling Publishers Pvt. Ltd.

Enjolras, B., Steen-Johnsen, K., & Wollebæk, D. (2013). Social media and mobilization to offline demonstrations: Transcending participatory divides? *New Media & Society, 15*(6), 890–908.

Esack, F. (2003). In search of progressive Islam beyond 9/11. *Progressive Muslims: On justice, gender, and pluralism* (pp. 78–97). London: Oneworld Publication, Inc.

Esposito, J. L., & DeLong-Bas, N. J. (2001). *Women in Muslim family law*. Syracuse, NY: Syracuse University Press.

Esposito, J. L., & Mogahed, D. (2007). *Who speaks for Islam? What a billion Muslims really think*. New York: Gallup Press.

Evans, P. (2012). *Counter-hegemonic globalization*. New York: John Wiley & Sons, Ltd.

Fahmy, M. (2011, November 19). Egyptian blogger Aliaa Elmahdy: Why I posed naked. CNN. Retrieved from www.cnn.com/2011/11/19/world/meast/nude-blogger-aliaa-magda-elmahdy/index.html

Fandy, M. (2007). *(Un)civil war of words: Media and politics in the Arab world*. New York: Greenwood Publishing Group.

FAO. (2017, March 15). Yemen needs urgent assistance to prevent famine. Retrieved from www.fao.org/news/story/en/item/522843/icode

Faraj, S., & Azad, B. (2012). The materiality of technology: An affordance perspective. In P. M. Leonardi, B. Nardi & J. Kallinikos (Eds.), *Materiality and organizing: Social interaction in a technological world* (pp. 237–258). NY City: Oxford University Press.

Fernea, E. (2010). *In search of Islamic feminism*. New York: Anchor.

Feroz, K., & Vong, S. (2014). Virality over YouTube: An empirical analysis. *Internet Research, 24*(5), 629–647.

Flew, T., & Smoth, R. (2014). *New media: An introduction*. Oxford: Oxford University Press.

Freeman, L. (1978). Centrality in social networks conceptual clarification. *Social Networks, 1*(3), 215–239.

Freeman, J., & Johnson, V. (1999). *Waves of protest: Social movements since the sixties.* Lanham, MD: Rowman & Littlefield.

Frison, E., & Eggermont, S. (2015). The impact of daily stress on adolescents' depressed mood: The role of social support seeking through Facebook. *Computers in Human Behavior, 44*, 315–325.

Furstenberg, F., & Hughes, M. (1995). Social capital and successful development among at-risk youth. *Journal of Marriage and the Family*, 580–592.

Gaby, S., & Caren, N. (2012). Occupy online: How cute old men and Malcolm X recruited 400,000 US users to OWS on Facebook. *Social Movement Studies, 11*(3–4), 367–374.

García Canclini, N. (1995). *Hybrid cultures: Strategies for entering and leaving modernity.* Minneapolis: University of Minnesota Press.

Ghanim, D. (2015). *The virginity trap in the Middle East.* New York: Palgrave Macmillan.

Ghosh, R., & Lerman, K. (2010). Predicting influential users in online social networks. arXiv preprint: arXiv:1005.4882.

Gibson, J. (1986). *The ecological approach to visual perception.* London: Psychology Press.

Giddens, A. (1990). *The consequences of modernity.* Stanford, CA: Stanford University Press.

Girls' Revolution. (2012a). Facebook. Retrieved from www.facebook.com/Revolution4Girls

Girls' Revolution. (2012b). Promo. YouTube. Retrieved from www.youtube.com/watch?v=-ewH6tS1Xpc

Girls' Revolution. (2012c). Monitoring harassment in the metro. YouTube. Retrieved from www.youtube.com/watch?v=W4ov1Kdp85o

Gitlin, T. (1998). Public sphere or public sphericules? In T. Liebes & J. Curran (Eds.). *Media, ritual, identity* (pp. 168–174). London: Routledge.

Goffman, E. (1976). *Gender advertisements.* New York: Harper Torchbooks.

González-Bailón, S., Borge-Holthoefer, J., & Moreno, Y. (2013). Broadcasters and hidden influentials in online protest diffusion. *American Behavioral Scientist, 57*(7), 943–965. doi:10.1177/0002764213479371

Gordon, S. (ed.). (2017). *Online communities as agents of change and social movements.* Hershey, PA: IGI.

Graham-Harrison, E. (2018, October 28). Social media "aids oppressors," says Saudi rights campaigner. *The Guardian.* Retrieved from www.theguardian.com/world/2018/oct/28/twitter-facebook-saudi-oppression

Grant, A., Guthrie, K., & Ball-Rokeach, S. (1991). Television shopping a media system dependency perspective. *Communication Research, 18*(6), 773–798.

Greenslade, R. (2016, December 24). Lawyers urge Egypt to lift travel ban on "Facebook girl" journalist. *The Guardian*. Retrieved from www.theguardian.com/media/greenslade/2016/dec/24/lawyers-urge-egypt-to-lift-travel-ban-on-facebook-girl-journalist

Grewal, R., Mehta, R., & Kardes, F. R. (2000). The role of the social-identity function of attitudes in consumer innovativeness and opinion leadership. *Journal of Economic Psychology*, *21*(3), 233–252.

Griffin, A. (2017, July 19). Sarahah: The top iphone app in the world is being used to bully people, users claim. *The Independent*. Retrieved from www.independent.co.uk/life-style/gadgets-and-tech/news/sarahah-app-iphone-ios-app-store-google-play-android-download-how-to-reviews-a7848801.html

Grindon, G. (2011). The notion of irony in cultural activism. In B. Firat & A. Kuryel (Eds.). *Cultural activism: Practices, dilemmas, and possibilities* (pp. 21–34). Amsterdam: Rodopi.

Groshek, J. (2014). Twitter collection and analysis toolkit (TCAT) at Boston University. Retrieved from www.bu.edu/com/bu-tcat

Gruhl, D., Guha, R., Liben-Nowell, D., & Tomkins, A. (2004, May). Information diffusion through blogspace. In Proceedings of the 13th international conference on World Wide Web (pp. 491–501).

The Guardian. (2017, March 8). Nike launches hijab for female Muslim athletes. Retrieved from www.theguardian.com/business/2017/mar/08/nike-launches-hijab-for-female-muslim-athletes

Haddad, Y. (1984). Islam, women and revolution in twentieth-century Arab thought. *The Muslim World*, *74*(3–4), 137–160.

Haddad, Y. Y., Smith, J. I., & Moore, K. M. (2006). *Muslim women in America: The challenge of Islamic identity today*. Oxford: Oxford University Press.

Hall, J. (2013, February 4). Saudi preacher who "raped and tortured" his five-year-old daughter to death is released after paying "blood money." *The Independent*. Retrieved from www.independent.co.uk/news/world/middle-east/saudi-preacher-who-raped-and-tortured-his-five-year-old-daughter-to-death-is-released-after-paying-8480440.html

Hall, A., & Wellman, B. (1985). Social networks and social support. In S. Syme & S. Cohen (Eds.). *Social support and health* (pp. 23–41). San Diego, CA: Academic Press.

Hall, S. (2001). Encoding/decoding. In M. Durham & D. Kellner (Eds.). *Media and cultural studies: Keyworks* (pp. 163–173). Oxford: Blackwell Publishing Ltd.

Halpern, D., & Gibbs, J. (2013). Social media as a catalyst for online deliberation? Exploring the affordances of Facebook and YouTube for political expression. *Computers in Human Behavior*, *29*, 1159e1168.

Hamdan, M. (2013, May 21). A sarcastic fatwa on air-conditioning is published in international media. Al-Madina. Retrieved from www.al-madina.com/article/230108

Hamelink, C. (1983). *Cultural autonomy in global communications*. London: Longman.

Harass Map. (2014). Sexual harassment in greater Cairo: Effectiveness of Crowdsourced data. Retrieved from harassmap.org/en/wp-content/uploads/2013/03/Towards-A-Safer-City_full-report_EN-.pdf

Hassaini, S. (2017, June 19). The Tunisian women who want to be virgins again. BBC Afrique. Retrieved from www.bbc.com/news/world-africa-40288822

Hassoun, Alma. (2018, March 27). Tara Fares: The murder of an Instagram star. BBC. Retrieved from www.bbc.co.uk/news/resources/idt-sh/tara_fares

Hayatouki. (2012, November 11). Turkish series are stealing wives. Retrieved from hayatouki.com/social-phenomena/content/1810037-سارقة-الزوجات-المسلسلات-التركية-سارقة-الزوجات#المسلسلات-التركية

Haythornthwaite, C. (2007). Social networks and online community. In *The Oxford handbook of internet psychology* (pp. 121–137).

Heath, J. (2008). *The veil: Women writers on its history, lore, and politics*. Oakland: University of California Press.

Heer, J., & Boyd, D. (2005, October). Vizster: Visualizing online social networks. In *IEEE Symposium on Information Visualization, 2005. INFOVIS 2005* (pp. 32–39).

Hesmondhalgh, David. (2013). *The cultural industries*. Thousand Oaks, CA: Sage.

Hilbert, M., Vásquez, J., Halpern, D., Valenzuela, S., & Arriagada, E. (2017). One step, two step, network step? Complementary perspectives on communication flows in Twittered citizen protests. *Social Science Computer Review, 35*(4), 444–461.

Hofstede, G. (1998). *Masculinity and femininity: The taboo dimension of national cultures* (vol. 3). Thousand Oaks, CA: Sage.

Hofstede, G., Hofstede, G. J., & Minkov, M. (1991). *Cultures and organizations: Software of the mind* (vol. 2). London: McGraw-Hill.

Hofstede, G. H., & Hofstede, G. (2001). *Culture's consequences: Comparing values, behaviors, institutions and organizations across nations*. Thousand Oaks, CA: Sage.

Hogan, B., & Quan-Haase, A. (2010). Persistence and change in social media. *Bulletin of Science, Technology & Society, 30*(5), 309–315.

Hopkins, N., & Solon, O. (2017, May 22). Facebook flooded with "sextortion" and revenge porn, files reveal. *The Guardian*. Retrieved from www.theguardian.com/news/2017/may/22/facebook-flooded-with-sextortion-and-revenge-porn-files-reveal

House, K. (2012). *On Saudi Arabia: Its people, past, religion, fault lines—and future*. New York: Knopf.

Huberman, B., Romero, D., & Wu, F. (2009) Social networks that matter: Twitter under the microscope. *First Monday*, 14.

Huckfeldt, R., Mendez, J. M., & Osborn, T. (2004). Disagreement, ambivalence and engagement: The political consequences of heterogeneous networks. *Political Psychology*, *25*, 65–95.

HuffPost—Arabi. (2017a, April 4). MBC apologizes for "#Be Fee" and takes steps against those responsible for it. Retrieved from www.huffpostarabi.com/2017/04/03/story_n_15787278.html

HuffPost—Arabi. (2017b, April 5). Saudi Tweeters force MBC to fire three employees due to "#Be Free#." Retrieved form www.huffpostarabi.com/2017/04/06/story_n_15835172.html

HuffPost—Arabi. (2017c, September 2). "Any girl who lost her virginity is a whore": False perceptions about Arab sexual literacy uncovered by the Moroccan writer Layla Al-Sulaimani. Retrieved from www.huffpostarabi.com/2017/09/02/story_n_17897994.html

Hui, P., Crowcroft, J., & Yoneki, E. (2011). Bubble rap: Social-based forwarding in delay-tolerant networks. *IEEE Transactions on Mobile Computing*, *10*(11), 1576–1589.

Hume, T. (2012, December 6). Silence over sexual violence: Arab women take stand on "absurd honor." CNN. edition.cnn.com/2012/12/06/world/meast/uprising-women-arab-world

Ibrahim, I. (1996). *Women's journalism in the Arab world*. Cairo: Al-Diwaliay House for Publishing and Dissemination.

Idriss, S. Z., Kvedar, J. C., & Watson, A. J. (2009). The role of online support communities: benefits of expanded social networks to patients with psoriasis. *Archives of dermatology*, *145*(1), 46–51.

ILDP (Iraq Legal and Development Program). (2006, December). The Status of women in Iraq: An update on assessing Iraq's observation of legal and actual international criteria. Retrieved from www.iraqi-alamal.org/uploads/pdf/pdf%202014/different%20pdf/iraq-status-of-women-update-arabic.pdf

Imam Bin Baz. (n.d.). Using the dish is a grave sin. Retrieved from www.binbaz.org.sa/article/220

Inglehart, R., & Norris, P. (2004). *Sacred and secular: Religion and politics worldwide*. Cambridge: Cambridge University Press.

Islamyat. (2013, April). The white ribbon: A campaign that targets Muslim women. Retrieved from islamyat.d1g.com/main/show/5234143

Itahawy, M. (2018, February 15). #MosqueMeToo: What happened when I was sexually assaulted during the hajj. *Washington Post*. Retrieved from www.washingtonpost.com/news/global-opinions/wp/2018/02/15/mosquemetoo-what-happened-when-i-was-sexually-assaulted-during-the-hajj/?utm_term=.55c134956979

Jalabi, R. (2014, August 11). Who are the Yazidis and why is Isis hunting them? *The Guardian*. Retrieved from www.theguardian.com/world/2014/aug/07/who-yazidi-isis-iraq-religion-ethnicity-mountains

Jastrow, M. (1921). Veiling in ancient Assyria. *Revue archéologique*, *14*, 209–238.

Jenkins, J. (1981). Resource mobilization theory and the study of social movements. *Annual Review of Sociology*, *9*, 527–553.

Johnston, H. (2014). *What is a social movement*? Oxford: John Wiley & Sons.

Juris, J. (2005). Networked social movements: Global movements for global justice. In M. Castells (ed.). *The network society: A cross-cultural perspective*. Cheltenham: Edward Elgar.

Kahn, R., & Kellner, D. (2004). New media activism: From the battle of Seattle to blogging. *New Media & Society*, *6*(1), 87–95.

Karam, A. (1998). *Women, Islamisms, and the State: Dynamism of power and contemporary feminisms in Egypt*. Hampshire: Macmillan Press.

Karaoğlan, B. (2007). Women's NGOs and their relations with the state in Egypt. Unpublished MA Thesis. Middle East Technical University, Turkey.

Karmi, G. (2005). Women, Islam and patriarchalism. In H. Moghissi (ed.). *Women and Islam: Images and realities*. London: Routledge.

Kashqari, Amira. (2013, May 3). What is hidden is worse. *Okaz* newspaper. Retrieved from okaz.com.sa/article/566277

Katz, E., & Lazarsfeld, P. (1955). *Personal influence: The part played by people in the flow of mass communications*. Glencoe, IL: The Free Press.

Katz, E. (1957). The two-step flow of communication: An up-to-date report on an hypothesis. *Public opinion quarterly*, *21*(1), 61–78.

Kavanaugh, A., Carroll, J. M., Rosson, M. B., Zin, T. T., & Reese, D. D. (2005). Community networks: Where offline communities meet online. *Journal of Computer-Mediated Communication*, *10*(4).

Keren, M. (2006). *Blogosphere: The new political arena*. Lanham, MD: Lexington Books.

Kerr, S. (2016, October 30). Romantic comedy puts spotlight on desires of Saudi youth. *The Financial Times*. Retrieved from www.ft.com/content/a17e85ac-9c3d-11e6-a6e4-8b8e77dd083a

Kempe, D., Kleinberg, J., & Tardos, É. (2003, August). Maximizing the spread of influence through a social network. In *Proceedings of the ninth ACM SIGKDD international conference on knowledge discovery and data mining* (pp. 137–146).

Khaleeli, H. (2010, April 15). Nawal El Saadawi: Egypt's radical feminist. *The Guardian*. Retrieved from www.theguardian.com/lifeandstyle/2010/apr/15/nawal-el-saadawi-egyptian-feminist

Khamis, S. (2010). Islamic feminism in new Arab media platforms for self-expression and sites for multiple resistances. *Journal of Arab & Muslim Media Research*, *3*(3), 237–255.

Khamis, S. (2011). The Arab 'feminist' spring? *Feminist Studies, 37*(3), 692–695.

Khamis, S. & Mili, A. (2017). *Arab women's activism and socio-political transformation: Unfinished gendered revolutions.* London: Palgrave Macmillan.

Khannous, T. (2011). Virtual gender: Moroccan and Saudi Women's cyberspace. *Hawwa, 9*(3), 358–387.

Khatab, S. (2006). *The political thought of Sayyid Qutb: The theory of jahiliyyah.* London: Routledge.

Khazen, J. (1999). Censorship and state control of the press in the Arab world. *Harvard International Journal of Press/Politics, 4*(3), 87–92.

Kim, J., & Lee, J. E. R. (2011). The Facebook paths to happiness: Effects of the number of Facebook friends and self-presentation on subjective well-being. *CyberPsychology, behavior, and social networking, 14*(6), 359–364.

Kim, H. (2014). Enacted social support on social media and subjective well-being. *International Journal of Communication, 8*, 21.

Kingsley, P. (2013, July 5). 80 sexual assaults in one day—the other story of Tahrir Square. *The Guardian.* Retrieved from www.theguardian.com/world/2013/jul/05/egypt-women-rape-sexual-assault-tahrir-square

Kollock, P. (1999). The economies of online cooperation. In M. Smith & P. Kollock (Eds.). *Communities in cyberspace* (p. 220). London: Psychology Press.

Kraidy, M. (2006). *Hybridity, or the cultural logic of globalization.* Philadelphia: Temple University Press.

Kraidy, M. (2016). *The naked blogger of Cairo: Creative insurgency in the Arab world.* Cambridge, MA: Harvard University Press.

Kurzman, C. (Ed.). (1998). *Liberal Islam: A source book.* Oxford University Press, USA.

Kwak, H., Lee, C., Park, H., et al. (2010) What is Twitter, a social network or a news media? *19th International Conference on World Wide Web.* New York.

Lakritz, T. (2017, June 16). 9 photos that show how album covers are censored in the Middle East. *Business Insider.* Retrieved from uk.businessinsider.com/women-album-covers-censored-middle-east-2017-6?IR=T/#kylie-minogues-entire-look-was-changed-3

LaRose, R., Mastro, D., & Eastin, M. S. (2001). Understanding internet usage: A social-cognitive approach to uses and gratifications. *Social Science Computer Review, 19*(4), 395–413.

Larsson, G. (2016). *Muslims and the new media: Historical and contemporary debates.* London: Routledge.

Lazreg, M. (2009). *Questioning the veil: Open letters to Muslim women.* Princeton, NJ: Princeton University Press.

Lee, E. (2013). Formation of a talking space and gender discourses in digital diaspora space: Case of a female Korean immigrants online community in the USA. *Asian Journal of Communication, 23*(5), 472–488.

Leistyana, P. (2008). Cultural activism. In T. Bennett & J. Frow (Eds.). *The SAGE handbook of cultural analysis* (pp. 697–716). Thousand Oaks, CA: Sage.

Leung, L. (2006). Stressful life events, motives for internet use, and social support among digital kids. *CyberPsychology & Behavior, 10*(2), 204–214.

Lewis, L. (2012). Convergences and divergences: Egyptian women's activism over the last century. In P. Arenfeldt & N. Golley (Eds.). *Mapping Arab women's movements: A century of transformations from within* (pp. 43–64). Cairo: American University of Cairo Press.

Li, X., Chen, W., & Popiel, P. (2015). What happens on Facebook stays on Facebook? The implications of Facebook interaction for perceived, receiving, and giving social support. *Computers in Human Behavior, 51*, 106–113.

Li, X. (2007). *Voices rising: Asian Canadian cultural activism.* Vancouver: UBC Press.

Lim, J. B. (2013). Video blogging and youth activism in Malaysia. *International Communication Gazette, 75*(3), 300–321.

Lin, C. (1999). Online-service adoption likelihood. *Journal of Advertising Research, 39*, 79–89.

Llewellyn-Jones, L. (2007). House and veil in ancient Greece. In *British School at Athens Studies* (pp. 251–258).

Lloyd-Davies, F. (2001, October 26). No compromise. BBC News. Retrieved from news.bbc.co.uk/2/hi/programmes/correspondent/1619902.stm

Lovejoy, K., & Saxton, G. (2012). Information, community, and action: How nonprofit organizations use social media. *Journal of Computer-Mediated Communication, 17*(3), 337–353.

Lu, W., & Hampton, K. N. (2017). Beyond the power of networks: Differentiating network structure from social media affordances for perceived social support. *New media & society, 19*(6), 861–879.

Macfarquhar, N. (2011). Saudis arrest woman leading right-to-drive campaign. *New York Times.* Retrieved from www.nytimes.com/2011/05/24/world/middleeast/24saudi.html

Mackey, R. (2015, February 12). Saudi women free after 73 days in jail for driving. *New York Times.* Retrieved from www.nytimes.com/2015/02/13/world/middleeast/saudi-women-free-after-73-days-in-jail-for-driving.html?_r=0

Macleod, S. (2007, May 10). 10 Questions for Queen Rania. *Time.*

Madani, D. (2012, October 16). Civil society initiative: The uprising of women in the Arab world. Association for Women's Rights in Development.

Majchrzak, A., Faraj, S., Kane, G. C., & Azad, B. (2013). The contradictory influence of social media affordances on online communal knowledge sharing. *Journal of Computer-Mediated Communication, 19*(1), 38–55.

Maktabi, R. (2011, October 4). Who are the Middle East's most influential women? CNN. Retrieved from edition.cnn.com/2011/10/04/world/meast/ime-women-call-out/index.html

Malkawi, L. (2013, April 6). Muslim women launch another campaign to counter Femen's "topless Jihad." Radio Sawa. Retrieved from www.radio-sawa.com/a/counter-campaign-femen-jihad-topless-muslim/221516.html

Mandaville, P. (2001). *Transnational Muslim politics: Reimagining the Umma*. London: Routledge.

Mandaville, P. (2003). Communication and diasporic Islam: A virtual Ummah? In K. H. Karim (ed.). *The Media of Diaspora* (pp. 135–147). London: Routledge.

Martin, J., Martins, R., & Wood, R. (2016). Desire for cultural preservation as a predictor of support for entertainment media censorship in Saudi Arabia, Qatar, and the United Arab Emirates. *International Journal of Communication, 10*, 23.

Massad, J. (2015). *Islam in liberalism*. Chicago: Chicago University Press.

Masliyah, S. (1996). Zahawi: A Muslim pioneer of women's liberation. *Middle Eastern Studies, 32*(3), 161–171.

MBC. (2013, January 21). Violence against women in Saudi Arabia: Beatings, dragging, running over by car, and food deprivation. Retrieved from goo.gl/3Z8DKQ

MBC. (2014, December 14). A Saudi Sheikh explains the reality of his interview with his wife on "Badriya" show on MBC. Retrieved from www.mbc.net/ar/programs/mbc-news/articles/ حقيقة-ظهور-زوجته-معه-في—بدرية—على-شيخ-سعودي-يوضح -MBC.html

McAdam, D., McCarthy, J. D., & Zald, M. N. (1996). *Comparative perspectives on social movements: Political opportunities, mobilizing structures, and cultural framings*. New York: Cambridge University Press.

McAdam, D., Tarrow, S., & Tilly, C. (2001). *Dynamics of contention*, New York: Cambridge University Press.

McEvoy, K., & McGregor, L. (Eds.). (2008). *Transitional justice from below: Grassroots activism and the struggle for change*. New York: Bloomsbury Publishing.

McLeod, J., Scheufele, D., Moy, P., Horowitz, E., Holbert, R., Zhang, W., & Zubric, J. (1999). Understanding deliberation: The effects of discussion networks on participation in a public forum. *Communication Research, 26*(6), 743–774.

McGuinness, D. (2017, August 7). The Berlin mosque breaking Islamic taboos. BBC News. Retrieved from www.bbc.com/news/world-europe-40802538

Meng, J., Martinez, L., Holmstrom, A., Chung, M., & Cox, J. (2017). Research on social networking sites and social support from 2004 to 2015: A narrative review and directions for future research. *Cyberpsychology, Behavior, and Social Networking, 20*(1), 44–51.

Merry, M. (2013). Tweeting for a cause: Microblogging and environmental advocacy. *Policy & Internet, 5*(3), 304–327.

Middle East Online. (2013, May 12). Campaign to stop domestic violence against women in Saudi Arabia: What is hidden is worse. Retrieved from www.middleeastonline.com/?id=155070

Mislove, A., Viswanath, B., Gummadi, K., & Druschel, P. (2010, February). You are who you know: Inferring user profiles in online social networks. In *Proceedings of the third ACM international conference on Web search and data mining* (pp. 251–260).

Moghadam, V. (2003). *Modernizing women: Gender and social change in the Middle East.* New York: Lynne Rienner Publishers.

Moradi, F., & Anderson, K. (2016). The Islamic state's Êzîdî genocide in Iraq: The Sinjār operations. *Genocide Studies International, 10*(2), 121–138.

Morrow, V. (1999). Conceptualising social capital in relation to the well-being of children and young people: A critical review. *The Sociological Review, 47*(4), 744–765.

Mortimer, Caroline (2017, June 7). Saudi Arabia jails human rights activist who defied women's driving ban. *The Independent.* Retrieved from www.independent.co.uk/news/world/middle-east/saudi-arabia-woman-driving-ban-jailed-loujain-al-hathloul-activist-a7777696.html

MTV Arabia. (2008a). MTV Arabia Bezer TVC. Retrieved from www.youtube.com/watch?v=cats9xoDhqo

MTV Arabia. (2008b). MTV Arabia Saudi TVC. Retrieved from www.youtube.com/watch?v=ok0Kp839RwI

Munro, E. (2013). Feminism: A fourth wave? *Political insight, 4*(2), 22–25.

Nabi, R. L., Prestin, A., & So, J. (2013). Facebook friends with (health) benefits? Exploring social network site use and perceptions of social support, stress, and well-being. *Cyberpsychology, Behavior, and Social Networking, 16*(10), 721–727.

Nah, S. (2009). Building social capital through nonprofit organizations' websites: Organizational features and e-social capital. Boston: AEJMC.

Nah, S., & Saxton, G. (2013). Modeling the adoption and use of social media by nonprofit organizations. *New Media & Society, 15*(2), 294–313.

Nahon, K., & Hemsley, J. (2013). *Going viral.* Oxford: Polity Press.

Nazra for Feminist Studies. (2011, February 20). Statement from the Coalition of Women's NGOs in Egypt. *Open Democracy.* Retrieved from www.opendemocracy.net/statement-from-coalition-of-womens-ngos-in-egypt

NCCI. (2011, April 28). Iraq's civil society in perspective—April 2011. Retrieved from www.ncciraq.org/en/archive/ncci-studies/item/download/2289_f329fbd71220ec90377e01f1eccbfacc

Nelson, S. (2013, April 5). Muslim women against Femen: Facebook group takes on activists in wake of Amina Tyler topless jihad. *The Huffington Post UK*. Retrieved from www.huffingtonpost.co.uk/2013/04/05/muslim-women-against-femen-facebook-topless-jihad-pictures-amina-tyler_n_3021495.html

The New Arab. (2017, April 25). Jordan axes controversial law allowing rapists to escape punishment. Retrieved from www.alaraby.co.uk/english/news/2017/4/25/jordan-axes-controversial-law-allowing-rapists-to-escape-punishment

Newman, M. (2005). A measure of betweenness centrality based on random walks. *Social Networks, 27*(1), 39–54.

New York Times. (2016, October 21). How Has Your Life as a Saudi Woman Changed? Retrieved from www.nytimes.com/2016/10/22/world/middle east/saudi-arabia-women.html?smid=tw-nytimesworld&smtyp=cur

Nihal, M. (2011, June 16). Virtual world has "real" problems. *Arab News*. Retrieved from www.arabnews.com/node/380884

Nobel Women's Initiative. (2011). Tawakkol Karman. Retrieved from nobelwomensinitiative.org/laureate/tawakkol-karman

Noble, S. (2018). *Algorithms of oppression: How search engines reinforce racism*. New York: New York University Press.

Norris, P. (2004). The bridging and bonding role of online communities. In P. Howard & S. Jones (Eds.). *Society online: The internet in context* (pp. 31–41). Thousand Oaks, CA: Sage.

Northwestern University in Qatar. (2013, June 18). Media use in the Middle East: An eight-nation survey by Northwestern University in Qatar. Retrieved from menamediasurvey.northwestern.edu

Nurmila, N. (2011). The influence of global Muslim feminism on Indonesian Muslim feminist discourse. *Al-Jami'ah: Journal of Islamic Studies, 49*(1), 33–64.

Obeidat, R. (2002). Content and representation of women in the Arab media. United Nations, Division for the Advancement of Women (DAW). Beirut, Lebanon November 12–15. Retrieved from www.un.org/womenwatch/daw/egm/media2002/reports/EP11Obeidat.PDF

O'Connor, P. (1992). *Friendships between women: A critical review*. Hertfordshire: Harvester Wheatsheaff.

Odine, M. (2013). Arab women use media to address inequality. *Journal of International Communication, 19*(2), 167–181.

O'Grady, S. (2015, November 24). Meet the comedian making Saudis laugh about driving laws. *Foreign Policy*. Retrieved from foreignpolicy.com/2015/11/24/meet-the-comedian-making-saudis-laugh-about-burkas-and-driving-laws

Olson, K. (2012). *Dress and the Roman woman: Self-presentation and society*. London: Routledge.

Oltermann, P. (2017, June 25). Liberal Berlin mosque to stay open despite fatwa from Egypt. *The Guardian*. Retrieved from www.theguardian.com/world/2017/jun/25/ibn-rushd-goethe-mosque-berlin-seyran-ates-egypt-fatwa-burqa-niqab?CMP=Share_iOSApp_Other

Osman, H. (2017, August 2). Laws that allow rapists to marry their victims come from colonialism, not Islam. *The Independent*. Retrieved from www.independent.co.uk/voices/rape-conviction-laws-marry-rapist-jordan-egypt-morocco-tunisia-came-from-french-colonial-times-a7872556.html

Otterbeck, J. (2008). Battling over the public sphere: Islamic reactions to the music of today. *Contemporary Islam*, *2*(3), 211–228.

Papanek, H. (1971). Purdah in Pakistan: Seclusion and modern occupations for women. *Journal of Marriage and the Family*, *33*(3), 517–530.

Park, S., Lim, Y., Sams, S., Nam, S., & Park, H. (2011). Networked politics on Cyworld: The text and sentiment of Korean political profiles. *Social Science Computer Review*, *29*(3), 288–299.

Pew Research. (2013). Among Muslims, internet use goes hand-in-hand with more open views toward Western culture. Pew Research: Religion and Public Life Project May 31. Retrieved from www.pewforum.org/2013/05/31/among-muslims-internet-use-goes-hand-in-hand-with-more-open-views-toward-western-culture

Postmes, T., & Brunsting, S. (2002). Collective action in the age of the internet: Mass communication and online mobilization. *Social Science Computer Review*, *20*(3), 290–301.

Preece, J. (2000). *Online communities: Designing usability supporting sociability*. Chichester: John Wiley and Sons.

Preece, J., & Maloney-Krichmar, D. (2003). Online communities: Focusing on sociability and usability. In J. Jacko & A. Sears (Eds.). *Handbook of Human-Computer Interaction* (pp. 596–620). Mahwah, NJ: Lawrence Erlbaum Associates.

Promundo & UN Women. (2017). Understanding masculinities: Results from the International Men and Gender Equality survey (images)—Middle East and North Africa Egypt, Lebanon, Morocco, and Palestine. Retrieved from promundoglobal.org/wp-content/uploads/2017/05/IMAGES-MENA-Executive-Summary-EN-16May2017-web.pdf

Radio Netherlands Worldwide. (2012, October 18). This autumn women launch their own Arab Spring. Retrieved from www.rnw.nl/africa/article/autumn-women-launch-their-own-arab-spring

Radsch, C., & Khamis, S. (2013). In their own voice: Technologically mediated empowerment and transformation among young Arab women. *Feminist media studies*, *13*(5), 881–890.

Rafael, V. (2003). The cell phone and the crowd: Messianic politics in the contemporary Philippines. *Philippine Political Science Journal*, *24*(47), 3–36.

Rane, H., & Salem, S. (2012). Social media, social movements and the diffusion of ideas in the Arab uprisings. *Journal of International Communication, 18*(1), 97–111.

Revolution against Patriarchal Society. (2012). Facebook. Retrieved from www.facebook.com/pages/ثورة-على-المجتمع-الذكوري/486472984703191

Rieder, B. (2013). Studying Facebook via data extraction: The Netvizz application. In WebSci '13 Proceedings of the 5th Annual ACM Web Science Conference (pp. 346–355). New York: ACM.

Rieder, B. (2015). YouTube Data Tools. *Computer software*. 1(0). Retrieved from tools.digitalmethods.net/netvizz/youtube

Riemersma, G., & van Tol, M. (2010, August 28). It's raining fatwas in Morocco this summer. Radio Netherlands Worldwide. Retrieved from www.rnw.nl/english/article/it%E2%80%99s-raining-fatwas-morocco-summer

Roberts, R. (2017, July 28). Tunisia: "landmark" new law gives women protection from rape and domestic violence. *The Independent*. Retrieved from www.independent.co.uk/news/world/tunisia-law-women-protect-rape-domestic-violence-north-africa-landmark-rights-abuse-sexual-a7864846.html

Robertson, R. (1992). *Globalization: Social theory and global culture* (vol. 16). Thousand Oaks, CA: Sage.

Roded, R. (ed.). (2008). *Women in Islam and the Middle East: A reader*. London: I.B. Taurus.

Róisín, F. (2015, August 28). The suffragettes of Saudi Arabia: "We try and be reasonable calling for our rights." *The Guardian*. Retrieved from www.theguardian.com/world/2016/may/03/saudi-arabia-gives-women-the-right-to-a-copy-of-their-marriage-contract

Rogers, E. (2010). *Diffusion of innovations*. New York: Simon and Schuster.

Rheingold, H. (1993). *The virtual community: Homesteading on the electronic frontier*. Reading, MA: Addison-Wesley Publishing.

Rodriguez, N. (2016). Communicating global inequalities: How LGBTI asylum-specific NGOs use social media as public relations. *Public Relations Review, 42*(2), 322–332.

Roy, O. (2004). *Globalized Islam: The search for a new Ummah*. New York: Columbia University Press.

Rubin, E. (2011, June 3). The feminists in Tahrir Square. *Newsweek*. Retrieved from www.newsweek.com/feminists-tahrir-square-66139

Sadiqi, F. (2006). Gender in Arabic. In *Encyclopedia of Arabic language and linguistics*. Leiden: Brill.

Sakr, N. (2007). *Arab television today*. London: I.B. Taurus.

Sakr, N. (2010). News, transparency and the effectiveness of reporting from inside Arab dictatorships. *International Communication Gazette, 72*(1), 35–50.

Saxton, G., Guo, C., Chiu, I., & Feng, B. (2012). Social media and the social good: How nonprofits use Facebook to communicate with the public. arXiv preprint arXiv:1203.5279.

Schaefer, C., Coyne, J. C., & Lazarus, R. S. (1981). The health-related functions of social support. *Journal of Behavioral Medicine, 4*(4), 381–406.

Schiller, H. (1975). Communication and cultural domination. *International Journal of Politics, 5*(4), 1–127.

Schwartz, S. (2008). *The other Islam: Sufism and the road to global harmony.* New York: Doubleday.

Segerberg, A., & Bennet, W. (2011). Social media and the organization of collective action: Using Twitter to explore the ecologies of two climate change protests. *The Communication Review 14*(3), 197–215.

Shaarawi, H. (1986). *Harem years: The memoirs of an Egyptian feminist, 1879–1924.* New York: The Feminist Press at CUNY.

Shaw, L., & Gant, L. (2002). In defense of the internet: The relationship between internet communication and depression, loneliness, self-esteem, and perceived social support. *Cyberpsychology & behavior, 5*(2), 157–171.

Siapera, E. (2012). *Understanding new media.* Thousand Oaks, CA: Sage.

Sidani, Y. (2005). Women, work, and Islam in Arab societies. *Women in Management Review, 20*(7), 498–512.

Sjoberg, L., & Whooley, J. (2015). The Arab Spring for women? Representations of women in Middle East politics in 2011. *Journal of Women, Politics & Policy, 36*(3), 261–284.

Smith, M. R., & Marx, L. (Eds.). (1994). *Does technology drive history? The dilemma of technological determinism.* Boston: MIT Press.

Smith, J. (1997). Doin' it for the ladies—youth feminism: Cultural productions/cultural activism. In Leslie Heywood & Jennifer Drake (Eds.). *Third wave agenda: Being feminist, doing feminism* (pp. 226–238). Minneapolis: University of Minnesota Press.

Smith-Spark, L. (2018, October 5). Denis Mukwege and Nadia Murad win Nobel Peace Prize for fight against sexual violence. CNN. Retrieved from www.cnn.com/2018/10/05/europe/nobel-peace-prize-intl/index.html

Snow, D., Soule, S., & Kriesi, H. (2008). Mapping the Terrain. In D. Snow, S. Soule, & H. Kriesi (Eds.). *The Blackwell companion to social movements* (pp. 3–16). Oxford: Blackwell Publishing.

The Social Call Committee. (1951). *The opponents and supporters of women's political rights.* Baghdad: Baghdad Printing Press.

Solomon, E., & Ghobari, M. (2011, October 7). Yemen Nobel laureate a figure of hope, controversy. Reuters. Retrieved from www.reuters.com/article/us-yemen-karman-nobel/yemen-nobel-laureate-a-figure-of-hope-controversy-idUSTRE79638920111007

Song, F. (2010). Theorizing web 2.0: A cultural perspective. *Information, Communication & Society, 13*(2), 249–275.

Southgate, D., Westoby, N., & Page, G. (2010). Creative determinants of viral video viewing. *International Journal of Advertising, 29*(3), 349–368.

Spencer, R. (2014, June 16). Iraq crisis: UN condemns "war crimes" as another town falls to Isis. *The Guardian*. Retrieved from www.telegraph.co.uk/news/worldnews/middleeast/iraq/10904414/Iraq-crisis-UN-condemns-war-crimes-as-another-town-falls-to-Isis.html

Spitzack, C., & Carter, K. (1987). Women in communication studies: A typology for revision. *Quarterly Journal of Speech, 73*, 401–423.

Sreberny-Mohammadi, A. (1997). The many cultural faces of imperialism. In P. Golding & P. Harris (Eds.). *Beyond cultural imperialism globalization, communication and the new international order* (pp. 49–68). Thousand Oaks, CA: Sage.

Stancati, M., & Al Omran, A. (2015, December 10). Saudi women to vote and run for first time in nationwide municipal election. *Wall Street Journal.* Retrieved from www.wsj.com/articles/saudi-women-to-vote-and-run-for-first-time-in-nationwide-municipal-election-1449784652

Stancati, M., & Said, S. (2018, November 20). Saudi Arabia accused of torturing women's-rights activists in widening crackdown on dissent. *Wall Street Journal.* Retrieved from www.wsj.com/articles/saudi-arabia-accused-of-torturing-women-activists-in-widening-crackdown-on-dissent-1542743107

Stanger, N., Alnaghaimshi, N., & Pearson, E. (2017). How do Saudi youth engage with social media? *First Monday, 22*(5).

Stewart, C. (2013, May 29). The new suffragettes: Courage in Cairo—the Arab women's awakening. *The Independent*. Retrieved from www.independent.co.uk/news/world/middle-east/the-new-suffragettes-courage-in-cairo-the-arab-women-s-awakening-8636534.html

Taboada, M., Brooke, J., Tofiloski, M., Voll, K., & Stede, M. (2011). Lexicon-based methods for sentiment analysis. *Computational linguistics, 37*, 267–307.

Taub, B. (2018, December 17). Iraq's post-ISIS campaign of revenge. *The New Yorker*. Retrieved from www.newyorker.com/magazine/2018/12/24/iraqs-post-isis-campaign-of-revenge

Thelwall, M. (2009). *Introduction to webometrics: Quantitative web research for the social sciences*. San Rafael, CA: Morgan & Claypool.

Tilly, Charles. (1978). *From mobilization to revolution*. Reading, MA: Addison-Wesley.

Thompson, E. (2001). Sex and cinema in Damascus. The gendered politics of public space in a colonial city. In H. Korsholm Nielsen & J. Skovgaard-Petersen (Eds). *Middle Eastern cities, 1900–1950: Public places and public spheres in transformation* (pp. 89–111). Aarhus N.: Aarhus University Press.

Toth, J. (2013). *Sayyid Qutb: The life and legacy of a radical Islamic intellectual.* Oxford: Oxford University Press.

Traboulsi, F. (2003). An intelligent man's guide to modern Arab feminism. *Al-Raida, 20*(100), 15–19.

Tremayne, M. (2014). Anatomy of protest in the digital era: A network analysis of Twitter and Occupy Wall Street. *Social Movement Studies, 13*(1), 110–126.

Tuchman, G. (1978). The symbolic annihilation of women by the mass media. In *Hearth and home: Images of women in the mass media*, G. Tuchman, A. Daniels, & J. Benet (Eds.). New York: Oxford University Press.

Tuchman, G. (1979). Women's depiction by the mass media. *Signs: Journal of Women in Culture and Society, 4*(3), 528–542.

Tucker, J. (2008). *Women, family, and gender in Islamic law*. Cambridge: Cambridge University Press.

UNDP. (2016). Human development report 2016: Human Development for Everyone. Retrieved from hdr.undp.org/sites/default/files/2016_human_development_report.pdf

UNHCR. (2014, July). WOMAN ALONE: The fight for survival by Syria's refugee women. Retrieved from www.unhcr.org/ar/53bb8d006.pdf

UNHCR. (2015, July 8). The 2014 global child protection, education and SGBV strategy implementation report. Retrieved from www.refworld.org/docid/559d1e124.html

UNICEF. (2011). Regional overview for the Middle East and North Africa: MENA gender equality profile status of girls and women in the Middle East and North Africa. New York: UNICEF. Retrieved from www.unicef.org/gender/files/REGIONAL-Gender-Eqaulity-Profile-2011.pdf

UNICEF. (2013). *Female genital mutilation/cutting: A statistical overview and exploration of the dynamics of change*. New York: UNICEF. Retrieved from www.unicef.org/media/files/UNICEF_FGM_report_July_2013_Hi_res.pdf

UNICEF. (2016, February 5). New statistical report on female genital mutilation shows harmful practice is a global concern. New York: UNICEF. Retrieved from www.unicef.org/media/files/FGMC_2016_brochure_final_UNICEF_SPREAD.pdf

United Nations. (2013). Combating domestic violence against women and girls: Policies to empower women in the Arab region. Retrieved from www2.unwomen.org/-/media/field%20office%20arab%20states/attachments/publications/2013/e_escwa_ecw_13_4_e.pdf?vs=3802

UN Women. (n.d.). Facts and figures. Retrieved from arabstates.unwomen.org/en/what-we-do/ending-violence-against-women/facts-and-figures

UN Women. (2013a). Regional consultation for the proposed general recommendation on women human rights in situations of conflict and post-conflict contexts: Arab states region state of art. Retrieved from www2.unwomen.org/-/media/field%20office%20arab%20states/attachments/publications/2015/regionalconsultationammanjan2013%20cedaw.pdf?vs=4528

UN Women. (2013b). Voices of women from the Arab states. Retrieved from www2.unwomen.org/-/media/field%20office%20arab%20states/attachments/publications/2013/unw%20voices%20of%20women%20from%20the%20arab%20states.pdf?vs=5547

UN Women. (2015). Progress of the world's women 2015–2016: Transforming economies, realizing rights. Retrieved from progress.unwomen.org/en/2015/pdf/UNW_progressreport.pdf

UN Women. (2015–2016). Annual report 2015–2016. Retrieved from www2.unwomen.org/-/media/annual%20report/attachments/sections/library/un-women-annual-report-2015-2016-en.pdf?vs=3016

Uprising of women in the Arab world. (2011a). About this intifada. Retrieved from uprisingofwomeninthearabworld.org/en/?page_id=1396

Uprising of women in the Arab world. (2011b). Who we are. Retrieved from uprisingofwomeninthearabworld.org/en/?page_id=1392

Valente, T., & Pumpuang, P. (2007). Identifying opinion leaders to promote behavior change. *Health Education & Behavior, 34*(6), 881–896. doi:10.1177/1090198106297855

Warren, A., Sulaiman, A., & Jaafar, N. (2014). Facebook: The enabler of online civic engagement for activists. *Computers in Human Behavior, 32*, 284–289.

Waterson, J. (2018, August 28). Saudi Arabia banned from advertising reform agenda on British TV. *The Guardian*. Retrieved from www.theguardian.com/uk-news/2018/aug/28/saudi-banned-from-promoting-its-reform-agenda-on-british-tv

Watson, N. (1997) Why we argue about virtual community: A case study of the Phish.Net Fan community. In S. Jones (ed.). *Virtual culture: Identity and communication in cybersociety* (pp. 102–132). Thousand Oaks, CA: Sage.

Watts, D. (2002). A simple model of global cascades on random networks. *Proceedings of the National Academy of Sciences, 99*(9), 5766–5771.

Watts, D., & Dodds, P. (2007). Influentials, networks, and public opinion formation. *Journal of Consumer Research, 34*(4), 441–458.

Wellman, B. (1979). The community question. *American Journal of Sociology, 84*, 1201–1231.

Wellman, B., & Wortley, S. (1990). Different strokes from different folks. *American Journal of Sociology, 96*, 558–588.

Weng, J., Lim, E., Jiang, J., & He, Q. (2010, February). Twitterrank: Finding topic-sensitive influential Twitterers. In *Proceedings of the third ACM international conference on web search and data mining* (pp. 261–270).

West, G., & Blumberg, R. (1991). Reconstructing social protest from a feminist perspective. In G. West & R. Blumberg (Eds.). *Women and social protest* (pp. 3–36). Oxford: Oxford University Press.

Wikileaks. (2007, February 3). Top five influential women in Iraq. Unclas Baghdad 000358. E.O. 12958. Retrieved from wikileaks.org/plusd/cables/07BAGHDAD358_a.html

Wikileaks. (2009, November 18). Yemen: Nomination for 2010 international women of courage award. Retrieved from wikileaks.org/plusd/cables/09SANAA2080_a.html

Winder, B. (2014). The hashtag generation: The Twitter phenomenon in Saudi society. Middle Eastern Studies Student Association. *Journal of Georgetown University-Qatar*, 6. doi:dx.doi.org/10.5339/messa.2014.6

Withnall, A. (2016, January 1). Isis "forced us to pray—then raped us": Yazidi survivor Nadia Murad describes life as a sex slave in northern Iraq. *The Independent*. Retrieved from www.independent.co.uk/news/world/middle-east/isis-forced-us-to-pray-then-raped-us-yazidi-survivor-nadia-murad-describes-life-as-a-sex-slave-in-a6792676.html

World Economic Forum. (2016). Insight report: The global gender gap of 2016. Retrieved from www3.weforum.org/docs/GGGR16/WEF_Global_Gender_Gap_Report_2016.pdf

Wu, J. (2014). Expanding civic engagement in China: Super girl and entertainment-based online community. *Information, Communication & Society*, *17*(1), 105–120.

Wu, P., & Wang, Y. (2011). The influences of electronic word-of-mouth message appeal and message source credibility on brand attitude. *Asia Pacific Journal of Marketing and Logistics*, *23*(4), 448–472.

YouTube. (2016, December 23). Majed Alesa-Hwages. Retrieved from www.youtube.com/watch?v=1rUn2j1hLOo

Yuce, S., Agarwal, N., Wigand, R., Lim, M., & Robinson, R. (2014, April). Studying the evolution of online collective action: Saudi Arabian women's "Oct26Driving" Twitter campaign. In *International conference on social computing, behavioral-cultural modeling, and prediction* (pp. 413–420). New York: Springer International.

Zachs, F., & Halevi, S. (2009). From Difāʿ al-Nisāʾ to Masʾalat al-Nisāʾ in greater Syria: Readers and writers debate women and their rights, 1858–1900. *International Journal of Middle East Studies*, *41*(4), 615–633.

Zald, M., & McCarthy, D. (Eds). 1987. *Social movements in an organizational society*. New Brunswick, NJ: Transaction.

Zhang, W. (2012). Virtual communities as subaltern public spheres: A theoretical development and an application to the Chinese internet. In H. Li (Ed.). *Virtual community participation and motivation: Cross-disciplinary theories* (pp. 143–159). Hershey, PA: IGI.

Zheng, Y., & Yu, A. (2016). Affordances of social media in collective action: The case of free lunch for children in China. *Information Systems Journal*. doi:10.1111/isj.12096

Zhou, H., & Pan, Q. (2016). Information, community, and action on Sina-Weibo: How Chinese philanthropic NGOs use social media. *VOLUNTAS: International Journal of Voluntary and Nonprofit Organizations*, *27*(5), 2433–2457.

Zimmerman, T. (2017). # Intersectionality: The fourth-wave feminist Twitter community. *Atlantis: Critical Studies in Gender, Culture & Social Justice*, *38*(1), 54–70.

Index

www.ingramcontent.com/pod-product-compliance
Lightning Source LLC
LaVergne TN
LVHW041111090826
844660LV00057B/204